THE OWL AND THE STEREO

AN INTRODUCTION TO RADICAL CHRISTIANITY

David Osborne

First Published 1997

ISBN 0 947988 99 8

Published by Wild Goose Publications

Wild Goose Publications, Unit 15, Six Harmony Row, Glasgow G51 3BA

Wild Goose Publications is the publishing division of the Iona Community.
Scottish Charity No. SC003794. Limited Company Reg. No SCO96243.

Distributed in Australia and New Zealand by Willow Connection Pty Ltd,
Unit 7A, 3-9 Kenneth Road, Manly Vale NSW 2093.

Permission to reproduce any part of this work in Australia or New Zealand
should be sought from Willow Connection.

A catalogue record for this book is available from the British Library.

Printed by The Cromwell Press Ltd, Melksham, Wilts.

TO TOM AND ELIE

ACKNOWLEDGEMENTS

A whole multitude of people have helped in this book:
students, teachers, writers, TV producers, and not least the many people
who have joined me in conversations and discussions over a number of years.
I am grateful to them all but would particularly like to thank:
my fellow church members who took part in the study course two years ago
from which the book developed; members of the Iona Community
who have encouraged me to produce it; and my family,
who have not only put up with me hogging the computer while I did it,
but even made encouraging noises as it happened.

Contents

Introduction
Double Focus

The Owl

Think of an owl. With that suggestion most of us probably think of the bird sitting in a tree, up close to the trunk and blinking at the world, like a picture of ancient wisdom. But an owl hunting at night is a very different picture. The owl's feathers enable it to fly almost silently; there is little turbulence around the wings. On the woodland floor a mouse moves; the owl locates it and closes in. As the mouse runs for cover the owl, even in darkness, follows its movement and if it cannot find shelter, the owl moves in for the kill. The owl tracks the mouse by both hearing and sight. Its eyes are sensitive to small amounts of light; so as long as there is not complete darkness the owl can see something. It can also hear the slightest rustle of the mouse's movements.

Like many hunting animals the owl locates its prey by using both eyes and ears. The eyes of the owl, like those of a human, face forward. This means that the two eyes see the same object but from slightly different positions. The brain is able to assimilate this data and work out the position of the object in a way that it could not do if the owl had one eye. In contrast, the eyes of many grazing animals are in the side of the head. This gives the animal a wide range of vision, which is helpful for alerting it to approaching danger. But it does not give it the same depth and precision as the hunter.

An animal's hearing works like the two eyes seeing the same object. The same sound is picked up by sensors in different positions. Again the brain is able to assimilate both signals and identify the source of the sound. If one eye or one ear does not work properly, the animal is disabled. Its ability to see and hear in depth is considerably reduced.

The Stereo

Now change the scene. The night-time hunting of the owl has gone on for hundreds of thousands of years. Move now to a commonplace situation which has emerged in the last thirty. A young man is lying across his bed flicking the pages of a magazine. There are posters on the wall and outside the window is the yellow glow of street lamps. The room is full of sound. Music comes from a small stereo on one side of the room and fills the room. It is not just loud, but spread out. The vocals are behind the lead guitar. The drums come from across the back, but the bass is coming from somewhere to the left. The sound recording has been carefully engineered. The sound emerges from two speakers but has been engineered so that it appears to come from across or around the room. With a mono recording from a single speaker the hearer is aware of the source of sound. But with good stereo one is 'in' the music.

This is like the owl's eyesight or hearing, but in reverse. The sound engineer mixes the recording so that the sound comes from two speakers fed from separate channels, to create a sound with a sense of space. With early stereo recordings this was done to reproduce the sound made by the band when they were performing. But now the recording engineer is generally producing a sound which has never actually been heard before. A person listening to a stereo may well hear music more clearly and with more depth than they would if they were listening to a live performance.

Double Focus

In the owl's case, its two eyes and ears give it a depth and accuracy of vision. With the loss of an eye or the hearing in one ear it would struggle to hunt and possibly not survive. In reproducing sound, two speakers can create a depth of sound which cannot be created with just one. And this can be developed further; putting four channels of sound through separate speakers in the corners of a room can mean that the listener is immersed in the music. This can serve as an analogy for what we will be doing in this book. Depth of vision requires looking at an object from two points at the same time and a full sound requires music from at least two different channels coming from separate speakers. In this book we will be, as it were, looking at the world from two different angles at the same time.

Think about it another way. The music from the stereo is more than just the sounds. The performers are probably not interested in how the engineer makes the sound. They will be interested in the end product, and in how well it sells. They will also be interested in the words, the mood and the feel of the music, what it is about and how people are going to feel or think when they hear it. Both the musician and the engineer are required to produce the recording. They are doing different things, with a different focus for their work, and together they make the record.

The hunting owl could be seen and described in a number of ways. It could be described in terms of the aerodynamics of its wing movements, the movement of its muscles or the way it uses its eyes and hearing to locate its prey. But someone could write a poem about the owl, trying to capture the power and grace of the owl's movement through the air. Someone else could write a poem or even a song about the owl moving in for the kill, seeing it not just as something that is happening between two animals in a wood somewhere, but as an image of a powerful and oppressive system stealthily closing in on the free individual; of the struggle for survival and the death of the weak.

In each case there is a different focus. It is possible to see and think about the whole world in terms of the mechanics of how it works. It is also possible to see it in terms of movement and pattern, of colour and shape and mood. Or it is possible to see it in terms of action, decision, value and meaning. People probably have their own preferences; certainly different kinds of work will call for a different emphasis.

There is also always the possibility of someone whose preference is for one way of seeing things ignoring or writing off the others as irrelevant or unreal. When that happens the person suffers, as something of what they could experience is closed off to them. In addition, other people or the world in general might suffer.

The Dancer

In some ancient Hebrew writings wisdom is the first creation of God, and like a child playing within the world. Wisdom could be thought of as like a dancer who both hears the rhythm and pattern of the music and is aware of their body and the space they are in.

If the dancer cuts either of these out, the dance falters. At times the dancer will not be deliberately thinking about the way their body is moving; training, practice, and instinctual ability enable the dancer to move without thinking how. At other times the dancer may not be deliberately hearing the music, but it is still there and the dancer responds to it unconsciously, moving to the music in the space around.

In this book we will have a double focus. One focus for our attention will be the way that we generally think about the world within Western society: how we have come to understand the nature of the universe we are part of; how we think about people and how they behave; how we respond to violence; and the whole activity of play and creative expression.

Generally our society is good at understanding and making things. It is less good at knowing how best to use the things that have been made. Working this out calls for another view of things which can enable us to see in depth, to locate the real issues and see not only what is possible, but what matters. For this our other focus will be the writings of the Hebrews and early Christians.

For various reasons the Hebrew and early Christian angle on life is often ignored within Western society. Sometimes this is because people think that they know what the Christian angle is and think they are living or working along those lines anyway. Some who believe that Western culture is leading the world towards a catastrophe see the Hebrew and Christian perspective as being the cause of the problem. Others simply believe that old views can have no relevance in a new period of history.

I do not believe it is that simple. The Church has not always been true to its roots and sometimes it has adopted attitudes and stances which are the exact opposite of what was called for by Jesus of Nazareth, and by the Hebrew prophets. The Christian Church has certainly had a profound influence on Western society, but Christianity has not been the only influence. And while in time people's ways of understanding the world and themselves change significantly, the world itself does not necessarily change so much, and neither do people. So it is always possible that someone of another time, and perhaps with a clearer, less cluttered view of life, saw things which we should take account of. I believe that to be the case with Jesus and the people whose writings came to be collected in the Bible.

Radical Christianity

I have called this book an introduction to radical Christianity because we will be concerned here with the roots of Christian faith. A while ago I moved house with my family. We cleared out a lot of boxes, cupboards and filing cabinets. A lot of stuff went to the skip or onto a bonfire and there was still enough left to fill a removal lorry. We took with us what we thought would be useful, some things we liked, and others which were souvenirs of good times in the past.

But occasionally I go backpacking. Then, when I decide what to take, I have to use a more radical approach. Every gram counts on a long walk, so the aim is to travel as light as possible. The question then is not, do I throw this away? But, what do I need to take? What is essential?

Radical Christianity begins with that kind of question. What is the Christian movement essentially about? As the churches may have wandered off course, what was the movement about in the beginning? The churches may have accumulated a lot of baggage on the way, so what is really basic to what they are about?

The same kind of questioning lies behind the way we consider the world we are part of, our understanding of ourselves and how we live. New insights are continually emerging into the international exchange of information through publishing, television, radio and the internet. But these are largely adding to, or amending, views which have come to be accepted in our society as basic. It is some of these basic and generally accepted views which we will be considering.

Like the dancer shifting focus from the music to the movement and back, we will try to bring these two perspectives together. Like the vision of the owl or the music from the stereo, the outcome will hopefully be a vision and sense of the world with depth and breadth: what people have sometimes called wisdom.

Using this Book

If you are planning a long journey you are likely to use maps with different scales. To get an overall picture of where you are going you will need a small scale map which shows a large area. Then, to get more detail, you use larger scale maps. This book is like a small scale map: it sketches out the land. To explore in more detail, read on elsewhere, talk with other people or read the basic sources for yourself. Use your own mind and ask your own questions. At the end of the book is a short list of books which might be helpful further reading.

This is not intended to be a handbook to life, the universe and everything. Applying a radical critique to society quickly brings to light a whole range of issues about power, sex, gender, race, trade, economics, community and more. Many of these we will only touch on indirectly if we refer to them at all. The aim of this introduction to radical Christianity is to provide a way of looking at the world which enables these matters to be addressed and a way of considering issues which can be applied in other situations. It may also give some suggestions as to how that might be done, and some pointers to where other people are already working in this way.

An individual chapter of the book might well make sense on its own. The first chapter introduces the idea of the Key Image, which is not necessarily referred to in all the later chapters, but which does explain what is going on in each one. The second is about the whole activity of learning, and the different kinds of learning we experience. This explains how it is that we can draw together insights from two very different cultures and times. The next five chapters deal with different issues and areas of understanding and action. The final chapter considers some of the key images of the first Christians, and what involvement in the Christian movement might mean.

So the book might not need to be read in order for parts of it to make sense, although I recommend reading the first two chapters before anything else. That should give an idea of what is going on in the later chapters. Reading the whole book should give an overview of a whole way of taking seriously now what Jesus and the first Christians were about.

CHAPTER ONE
KEY IMAGES

OVERVIEW

Galileo and the New World View

Sometime in 1609 Galileo saw what no-one on earth had seen before. He had heard that in Flanders an instrument had been made using lenses which could make distant objects seem much nearer. Having heard of the idea he worked out for himself how it was done and built his own telescope.

Once he had it up and working, Galileo demonstrated it to the leading citizens of Venice. It was a success. Not only did it amaze people, but it also had economic importance: traders and dealers would now be able to recognize ships approaching the harbour when they were twenty miles away; deals could be struck in anticipation of the ships arriving, and preparations could be made for dealing with their possible cargoes. Money could be made from the telescope.

Then, when the dealers of Venice were satisfied, Galileo started working with the telescope on his own interests. He boosted its magnification and looked at the sky, and he saw stars no-one had ever seen before. There in the darkness between the constellations were more stars, great sweeps of lights, minuscule but dramatic. He also looked at the moon and saw mountains, valleys and craters. He saw it as a great sphere of rock, like the earth.

This new view of the sky convinced him of something he had suspected for some time. As well as the telescope, a new idea had come from the north of Europe — that the earth was not at the centre of the universe but was moving in space around the sun. Nicholas Copernicus had come up with the idea and supported it with calculations. Most people thought he was mad but that was what his mathematics seemed to show him.

Copernicus's idea was not really new. Some Greek astronomers had thought the same thing but had not been able to prove it, and their ideas had disappeared into the dustbin of history. In the Middle Ages in Europe it was thought that the earth was the centre of the cosmos. That was what was in the Bible. It fitted in with what philosophers like Aristotle had said, and it appealed to common sense. The sun rose in the morning and set in the evening. The stars moved across the sky in regular patterns. God was concerned about humanity, so humanity's home must be the centre of his attention and of the universe.

Then it became clear that the earth was not flat but was actually round. Columbus had had trouble getting backing for his project of sailing into the sunset and coming round the other side, but eventually he got it. He did not succeed but sailed into the West Indies instead and opened another chapter of European history in another continent. But Magellan's crew did it and others followed. Gradually it became accepted that the world was round, even if the idea did seem odd and hard to believe.

Strangely, this did not cause an enormous stir in religious circles, even though in the opening chapter of the Bible the earth is made as a solid stand of rock with a dome of sky over the top of it. If it was a sphere, the earth could still be at the centre of things; religious thinkers could accommodate this change.

Even when it was proved that the earth was spherical there was still a significant problem for astronomers. The difficulty was the planets. The stars moved in smooth arcs across the sky, the variations in the path of the sun had been known for millennia and marked off in standing stones way back in the mists of time, but the planets were an oddity. In their paths across the sky they looped back on themselves, forming a smooth but complicated pattern and they all behaved differently. Some moved in big loops, others in smooth arcs with occasional hiccups; their movement was rhythmical, but it was complicated.

In the later Middle Ages people loved clockwork. Great cathedrals acquired clocks which told not only the hour and the minute but the phases of the moon and the length of day. All this could be built into a great mechanical timepiece. But this was not the case with the planets. In 1350 a man called Giovanni de Dondi did make a clock showing the paths of the planets, but it required seven dials to show them. No-one could make it simpler than that, and to astronomers, mathematicians and clockmakers that was something of an irritation. And then Copernicus had his bright idea.

One of the things that artists had begun to do was to draw or paint objects from several angles, and explore the whole business of perspective. Copernicus did that in his head with the mathematics of the paths of the planets, and came up with a new solution. He put the moon going round the earth and the earth and the planets going round the sun in a circle, and it all came out neatly. Quite neatly. Everything did not quite fit, but it was a lot neater than the previous idea, so Copernicus made his theory public.

The public did not think much of the idea. They were not used to having scientists tell them on the basis of some calculations that what they could see with their own eyes was wrong. But Copernicus survived. He was living in Northern Europe at a time when there was a burst of new thinking and the hold of the Catholic Church over intellectual life had been weakened. A new way of reading the Bible was leading some people to break away from the Catholic Church. Martin Luther, a leader of this new movement, thought Copernicus was a fool, but it was a place and a time when new ideas were in the air, and people could get away with them; a few people thought Copernicus might be right.

One person who thought that Copernicus was right was Galileo, down in Northern Italy. But, apart from the calculations, there was nothing else to go on. The old idea was obviously hard to hold on to. The new idea seemed to fit better. But when Galileo pointed his telescope at the sky, and saw stars stretching off into space and the moon like another earth, and watched other moons circling round other planets, he was convinced. Copernicus was clearly correct, and when anyone looked at it the way Galileo had, with his new instrument, they were likely to agree. Galileo too made his theory public.

He was not as lucky as Copernicus. He was not living in the turmoil of ideas of Northern Europe, with freethinking Germans and Dutch people. He was in Italy and had to contend with a Catholic Church which was becoming increasingly paranoid. The breakaway churches in the North were clearly not coming back into the fold. The Armada against England had failed. The whole marvellous edifice of church organization and intellectual control which had developed through the Middle Ages had had two centuries of knocks, and now a century of cracking and breakages. The Church's intellectual engineers were working flat out to keep at least some of the building together, and they turned their attention to Galileo. He was quizzed by the Inquisition, achieved nothing in appealing to the Pope and, after veiled threats and a house arrest, he said he was wrong and retired quietly.

But gradually his view came to be accepted. Johannes Kepler in Prague tidied up the mathematics, drawing the paths of the planets as ellipses rather than circles, and having the planets move at a speed that varied according to how far they were from the sun. More and more people came to be able to look through telescopes and see first the moon resembling a small earth, and then planets, some with their own moons. People continued to talk about the sunrise and the sunset, because as far as they were concerned that was what the sun did, but they also came to accept that it was actually us on our planet moving around the great sun.

Newton's Principles

Another change came in the next generation. One of the unanswered questions had been how it was that the planets, including the earth, continued to move around the sun without slowing down, shooting off into space, or crashing into each other. It was somehow connected to the question of why things fall down to the earth when they are dropped.

There was an old explanation of this but it became gradually less acceptable. This explanation was that things returned to the earth when dropped because that was where they came from in the first place. If you pick up a stone from the ground and drop it, it falls because its natural inclination is to go back to the ground from which it was lifted, in the same way that swallows return to their nests, travel-sick sailors want to go home and the soul yearns for God from whom it came. But this was harder to accept when the earth was no longer thought of as the great mass around which all else moved.

Isaac Newton saw another possibility. Legend has it that this happened when he saw an apple fall to the ground. Whether or not that is the case is not known, but in the same way that Copernicus suddenly looked at things from another angle, so did Newton. Instead of thinking about an apple falling to the ground he thought about an apple and the earth moving towards each other. The earth was so big that its movement was negligible, or effectively zero; the apple, being small, moved easily, and fell to the ground. What he saw instead of the apple being attracted to the earth was the apple and the earth being attracted towards each other. He then worked out the details.

According to Newton the force of attraction between two bodies was dependent on their mass and their distance apart. Bodies also continued to move in a straight line unless something pushed or pulled them another way. The planets continued to move around the sun because, although left to their own devices, they would carry on moving out into space in a straight line — they were being pulled by the sun. Like a conker on a string being whirled around a child's hand, the planets whirl round and round the sun. The force of gravity is like the string, pulling the planets towards the sun, with enough force to stop them moving out into space, and not enough to make them move towards the sun. The whole system is in balance.

Newton was a cautious man who worked out all sorts of things which he never published, but he was persuaded to write all this out. It took him three years to do it, with a lot of encouragement from friends and colleagues. It was published as *The Mathematical Principles of Natural Philosophy*, and was his major work on mechanics, motion and gravity. The book was often called the *Principia*, from its Latin title. The contents became known as Newton's Laws of Motion and his Law of Universal Gravitation. Later, generations of astronomers, engineers and physicists used what he had worked out. Unlike Galileo, Newton's ideas were accepted by the new intellectual establishment and he became a respected and influential man in British society at the time of Queen Anne.

The fact that it took Isaac Newton three years to write the *Principia* is significant. He was a solitary and secretive man who seemed to be afraid that other people were going to steal his ideas. He was also hard working and brilliant, becoming a professor at Cambridge when he was twenty six. The problem was the amount of work involved in producing the detailed mathematical arguments that needed to go into the *Principia*. Newton had seen what was going on, and done some calculations. This was enough to convince other people as well. Other mathematicians and scientists were sure Newton was right; they had seen it too. But they did not have the detail, and that took a long time to produce.

The significant thing here is that the insight came first, and then the detailed argument. The insight was a way of looking at things. This was the case literally, looking at an apple and the earth as drawn to each other rather than the one to the other, and conceptually, where in his mind Newton had a pattern of ideas about forces and movement. Newton saw the solution before he worked out the argument.

Key Images

Characters like Newton and Copernicus are exceptions in history. They had new ways of seeing things which in time came to affect the way that millions of others saw or thought about their world. However, they were not exceptions in the way that they went about things or in the way they influenced others. Although the details were complicated the basic process was simple.

There was an old idea which had become steadily less tenable with new information. It had become like a rickety building, with cracks in the walls, and even slipping in the foundations. But people stayed with it as they had no better idea. Then someone came up with another idea, which came from another way of seeing things. The new way of seeing fitted the new situation and in time other people came to accept it. The old way of seeing passed away; the new had arrived.

But the new did not arrive fully developed. It came as a way of seeing things: an alternative view; a new pattern. It was not as if someone had built a new house, complete with all its fittings and everyone thought this was much nicer than the old shack they had. It was as if an architect had given them a vision of another way of using their materials, reshaping things and putting them together differently. Once they had got the vision they knocked down the old structure and started on the new one.

It seems that this is the way that we come to think about things, or to stay with the ideas we have. It is not that we have everything sorted out in our minds, all hanging together, neat and tidy, but that we have in our minds a number of images around which other ideas move. Amidst all the things we think and believe there are some key images which provide us with a particular way of seeing the world. Other things we think or believe then fit in with them. These significant images are like the key of a piece of music which suggests the way that the notes are going to blend together, and provide the mood and possibilities of the tune. Or they are like the keys of cupboards which undo the locks and open the doors. Or they are like a crucial stone in an old building which holds others together in an arch.

In time Copernicus's way of seeing the planets moving round the sun became not only a key image for astronomers but for other people as they thought about the world they lived in. Newton's view of objects attracting each other being moved by gravity became a key image for generations of physicists and engineers.

In the philosophy of science these key images are referred to as 'paradigms'. They are significant ideas or models — ways of visualizing or making sense of an array of data — which set in train a whole host of ways of interpreting more information. Copernicus provided a new paradigm as did Newton and, later, did Darwin, Freud, Einstein and Mendel, and many others who broke new ground in scientific development but are less well known. But paradigms, and other key images, are not only used by scientists.

When politicians want to promote a programme or policy they do not pour out all the detailed argument at everybody. They devise a slogan or coin a soundbite and hope this will capture the imagination of their hearers and lead them into their way of seeing things and accepting their ideas. Advertisers also go for a slogan or a visual image which they hope will convince the public of the value of the product.

Key images also play a significant part in the values of individuals and societies. An American minister was trying to explain to a group of English students how American religion differed from that of England. 'You have to remember,' he said, 'the picture of the pioneer setting off into the wilderness on the wagon train. That is the dominant image of American religion: taming the wilderness. There's no wilderness left now, they've filled it up with beer cans, but that is what it is about.'

To explain English religion to an American, one would point out that in almost any bookshop in England there will be some glossy publications on English villages. These will have on the cover a photograph of the typical English village with a pub, cottages, a village green and a church. There will always be a church tower. It is so much a part of English culture that most people do not notice it, but similar books about Scotland or Wales will not have church towers. The village and the church are key images which affect how English people feel about the land they live in, and if they are at all inclined to think about religion, these images, there in their minds and reinforced by a hundred advertisements, calendars and book covers, will affect their thoughts about Christianity.

A key image will often be an actual memory for people . This may not be a recalling of how things really were as far as measurable data is concerned, but it is how things were for them. A place they went on holiday might be 'a miserable place': it was raining and they went into a pub there and the landlord was rude and the beer was poor; there were some youths shouting over the noise of a jukebox and the ashtray was full of cigarette butts. They do not want to go there again.

The whole of Bognor might not be like that at all. It might often be sunny, and the people might be friendly, but the memory is there and will affect any decisions they make about going back to Bognor. Even if they realize it is not reasonable to write off a place on the basis of one brief experience, it will still affect their emotions and their decision making, and sometimes only a new and very different experience will alter things. They might decide to rise to the challenge and give Bognor another try, but if they found things different in Torquay they are more likely to go there again.

Other key images are provided by significant figures in people's early lives. It might be that these figures become role models against which other teachers, mothers, fathers or leaders are measured, or against which people measure themselves. Or the key image may be provided by this person's words or attitudes. Someone whose father frequently made a particular statement about Labour voters, Tory voters, trade unions or lager drinkers is likely to be influenced by this for a long time. The words of the father, the mother, or other person of influence can become, as a slogan, a key image for making judgements and decisions. A person might react against it, or go with it, but it is likely to have an influence one way or another.

The Power of Myth

One very significant but also very subtle form of key image is the myth. In general use the word often means something that is not true, but in religious studies it has a specific and positive meaning. In the study of religion a myth is a story which has a significant role in affecting people's behaviour and thinking; the story may or may not be historically true. What makes it a myth is its influence and importance.

The story of the Exodus from Egypt is a myth for Jewish people which has come to affect their festivals, prayers and behaviour, and their whole sense of who they are. The story of the gunfight at the OK Corral is a myth for American society, and the rescue of the British Expeditionary Force from Dunkirk has become one for Britain. Myths are stories which are key images for a group of people. It is this influence that makes it a 'myth', whether or not the event actually happened.

The concept of myth is important for both religious studies and sociology. It is unfortunate that the word 'myth' is also often used in other settings to mean something which is not true, or something which is only true occasionally. People say, 'It's just a myth,' when they mean it is not something to be taken seriously. Not surprisingly this can lead to misunderstandings so that theologians talking about 'the Myth of the Resurrection' are heard to be suggesting they do not believe in the Resurrection. What they are actually talking about is the fact that the story of the resurrection of Jesus affects the way that Christians think about and feel about life. Such a story is a key image for Christians.

Another key image may be a scene, or a setting for a story. For some people Paris conjures up The Romantic Weekend; Milan – the Opera; the Isle of Man – a vision of motorbikes; Majorca – hot beaches. Places like Wembley, Skye, Oxford, Derry, Cardiff Arms Park, Westminster, the Gorbals, the City are for many people much more than names of places. The words draw up ideas, dreams, images and memories which are significant for their own sense of who they are and for their hopes.

In England the village is like that for many people. It is not a particular village, but any village, or at least a 'proper' village. This has a village green, a pub, cottages and a church. It also has a lot of people who have a sense of belonging to the place, and who get on with each other, arguing from time to time but also supporting each other in difficulties. The village is seen as a little hub of community.

This leads many English people who have lived all their lives in towns or suburbs to hanker for a place in the country, where they can not only look at fields and trees but also have a local community with other villagers. When the opportunity arises they move into a village, and then some are disappointed. There is not only a shortage of the facilities which they took for granted in their urban home, but also a lack of that indefinable something called 'village life' which they had expected to find and enter into. Others are fortunate and do find something of what they lacked in the town.

The significant thing here though is that the English village acts as a kind of mini-myth, affecting the hopes and aspirations of people who only actually experience English country life on occasional holidays and Sunday outings. The village acts as a key image for many people in England. For other people it may not be a particular place, like those just mentioned, but it may be a general setting which evokes for them hopes and aspirations: the stage or a film studio; a sailing boat or a caravan; the open road; a sandy beach; a forest or mountains.

Difference and Change

In Western society many key images vary from person to person. There are different political parties and religious movements, various styles of music and clothing; and people have different dreams of the good life, and different ambitions and standards of success. Other key images are widespread and have become generally accepted within Western society. Most accept that the earth moves round the sun and, however little they understand it, believe that it is gravity which keeps the planets in their course, or at least stops them flying off this particular spinning planet.

Key images also change from time to time. With the more individual images this can be seen happening; fashions change, political trends ebb and flow, and people's hopes alter as time goes on. With the more widely held ones the change is slower; major shifts in outlook, like those that took place in the times of Galileo and Newton, happen less often. They also happen slowly, seeping into society's consciousness rather than breaking in suddenly. While the fortunes of a political party might turn within a week and new images for summer clothing change from year to year, the big changes in outlook happen more slowly, as people gradually take on new ways of seeing things.

All kinds of change can be difficult. An old idea, even if it does not fit new information very well, is at least familiar and can be found to have some things to commend it. A new idea will have a knock-on effect which cannot often be anticipated so new ideas generate anxiety. They might solve puzzles in some areas, but create uncertainties in others. The fact of the change also creates a sense of anxiety: the old way of seeing things turned out to be wrong; perhaps other old ideas were also mistaken; maybe the new one will also be a mistake.

This anxiety can hover around the everyday decisions of life. What shall we eat? They used to say butter was bad for us, but now they seem to be saying it is good. What shall we drink? They used to say red wine was not a good thing, but now they are saying it can help fend off heart disease. What shall we wear? How can I maintain my credibility with these old clothes in my wardrobe?

The slow changes perhaps generate less anxiety because most people are not aware of what is happening. But those who do see, and can guess where these changes might lead, can become afraid. This was the case with those who silenced Galileo. The same was happening in the nineteenth century when people tried to stop the promotion of evolutionary ideas and amongst religious people in the following century who wrote off all psychology as nonsense. This was the anxiety of change on a big scale.

The ebb and flow of opinion can lead people to cry out for certainty, for a fixed point in all the changes. People sometimes hanker for a way of seeing things which they know to be right, which is not questioned, but is absolutely true. There seems no shortage of emergent leaders and religious movements who will claim to provide that. There are groups which claim infallibility for their holy book or their teacher. Amongst some Christians the Bible is promoted as the inspired Word of God, to be read as words dictated by God through the writers, not to be questioned but simply interpreted. For most Muslims the Koran has that status. There are smaller groups whose leader or guru provides the certainty people crave.

The Roman Catholic Church silenced Galileo but eventually lost the argument about the solar system. As ideas and opinions have developed with increasing speed in Western society the Roman Church has slowly centralized its control of church teaching. The doctrine of Papal Infallibility was only put forward in the nineteenth century.

There was a variety of opinion in the Catholic Church in the Middle Ages which would not be tolerated now. Similarly the concept of the verbal inerrancy of Scripture which is held by some Protestants had no place in the thinking of the Church in its first centuries.

The Original Context

The Christian movement began in a society not unlike our own. Technologically and politically the world of the Roman Empire was very different from that of present day Europe, but it was a society in which there was a variety of opinion and belief about the nature of the world, about human nature and society, and about gods and superhuman powers.

Rome had political control over Western Europe and the Mediterranean basin. Within that area, and often living together in the same cities, were people with a whole range of opinions, beliefs and religious practices. All that Rome required was allegiance or obedience to the Empire. As long as people made the necessary signals of respect, or did not cause trouble, they could believe what they liked. And they believed all sorts of things.

The first Christians wanted to communicate to others their experiences of God and the world. Sometimes they spoke with people of the same cultural background as themselves, with common assumptions and concerns. But the movement also spread across cultural boundaries, amongst Jews of different persuasions, Samaritans and monotheistic Greeks, and then amongst others whose religious background was in Stoic philosophy, or the cults of Isis, amongst Mithraists, Platonists, pagan Celts, a multitude of other religions and also among people who had little time for religious niceties.

The Christians' religious writings and practices developed as they tried to make connections between their way of seeing things and that of the people around them, and to make sense of their own lives in the light of what they had come to believe about God. Their beliefs did not arrive, fully developed, to be passed on safely to the next generation, but they emerged in the intellectual and spiritual struggle of living with Christian faith in a very mixed and varied society.

While the Christians did not become a totally separate group from the rest of society, their faith, with its accompanying attitudes and values, did distinguish them in many ways. As time went on and they

were sometimes treated as an odd or dangerous minority, they became a distinctive group. They sometimes met in secret and only introduced others to their central rites of Baptism and Communion when
they had received a long and intensive preparation.

However, their faith was something they held within an intellectual
framework which they shared with many of their neighbours. There
were various kinds of Jewish Christians, there were Samaritan Christians, and other Christians who understood the world in Stoic or
Platonist terms, or in a similar way to many of the other various cults
of the time which looked for salvation from the destructive powers of
the world. The Christians were not one group with one way of seeing
things, totally at odds with the rest of their society. They were a number
of different groups distinguished from, but also sharing much with,
the people amongst whom they lived.

Therefore, Christians now who try to interpret or understand their
faith within the basic way of seeing things of their own society, are in
line with what others were doing in the first centuries of the Christian
movement. They will perhaps use different terms and images from
many Christians of an earlier time, but be true to what those earlier
Christians were doing.

Living in Boxes

When it became generally accepted that Copernicus and Galileo were
right, and the earth did move round the sun, the Church did not re-
write its creeds and service books. The Church continued to celebrate
Jesus going up into heaven on Ascension Day, it continued to sing
'glory to God in the highest' and refer to the earth being founded
upon the waters. That was fair enough. What had perhaps for some
people been literal language now became poetic imagery, like the talk
about the sunrise but with rather more significance.

This was not new. For centuries the Church had been singing psalms
about the tribes going up to Zion, even though the Israelite tribes had
stopped going to Jerusalem on Mount Zion in AD 70. In the early
days of Christianity, Zion had ceased to be a particular place but had
stayed as an image of the presence of God. The picture of Israelites
going up to Zion to worship had always had something poetic about
it, and had been an inspiring vision more than a description of historical or geographical events. Now it became more poetic; it became

even more of a spiritual vision and even less a description of the physical world. The same thing could, and did, happen as people's way of seeing, and understanding, the world changed.

A difficulty with this was that in some ways it became harder for the spiritual vision to have an impact on people when they were outside the confines of worship. In the church service they could sing it and believe it. In the church, their image of the world could be of a ladder of reality rising up through ranks of angels to God in the highest place of the heavenly realm, and of God the Son descending to the lowest places of the earth, where they struggled for survival or love in the mess of everyday life. They might think and speak of God pouring out his Spirit on the church below, to enable it to live the life of faith and finally be raised to the heavenly places.

But in that mess of everyday life the vision could fade. Regular prayer and returns to the house of prayer might restore the vision, but it might not. The words might become empty and the vision of glory feel like little more than a pleasant daydream. One might wish to recapture it, but one might also suspect that it was all wishful thinking.

Amongst those who continue the life of prayer and worship there can develop a double life, with a double view of the world. Within the confines of church life and, particularly when taking part in its worship, the Christian view of the world can seem to make sense. It can give hope, meaning and encouragement, and generate a love for other people. But it might only actually make sense whilst an outdated way of looking at the world is maintained. Outside this context it is not disbelieved, but does not really relate to other things that need doing, and to other ways of thinking about the world.

The outcome of this is church congregations which can join together in worship. The members are able to discuss what they believe with each other, but they have great difficulty in talking about what they believe with people who are not part of that community of faith. They also have great problems in trying to relate what they believe within the context of the Church, to the kind of things they do every day in their work or their home life.

This is the state of a great many churches at the present time. It is as true of churches which are alive and flourishing as it is of those which appear to be in the last stages of some dire disease. Lively and imaginative ministers can stoke up the fires of conviction in the bible study or the sermon, and they can move people with the liturgy. If they have a strong sense of authority they can help the congregations feel safe in a changing and confusing world. But the members struggle to make connections between their Christian beliefs and the mundane issues of their lives, and are often extremely uncomfortable talking about their beliefs with people who do not share them. It is as if they live in two boxes, and what belongs in one box does not fit comfortably in another.

Making Connections

This is the issue we will be dealing with in the following chapters. In line with the first Christians who tried to make sense of their faith within the basic way of understanding the world and themselves which their culture provided, we will try to make some sense of Christianity within the way of seeing things which is now widely shared in Western society.

The whole cosmos is now generally thought of as an expanding universe, and life on this planet as an interconnection which has developed over millions of years. We will try to relate this to the Christian and Jewish idea of the world as God's creation. We will also consider one widely accepted psychological view of how we become the people we are, and see how that relates to the teaching and attitudes of Jesus.

From there we will move on to think about Jesus' way of dealing with violence, and compare that with the usual ways of dealing with threat and conflict within Western society. We will then consider the fundamental human activity of playing, and what the Bible calls the life of the 'Spirit'. That will bring us back to the issues of prayer and worship. Finally we will look at some of the language about God and Jesus which has been used by Christians since the early days of the movement, and think about what is meant by 'faith'.

In doing this we will consider a number of influential key images and relate them to key images which are a part of the traditional Christian understanding of God and the world. The aim is to try to develop a Christian way of thinking about the world which does not lead to life being lived in separate compartments, but as a whole.

In terms of the images introduced at the beginning of this book, we could say that we will aim to bring together two different ways of seeing the world so that they give a depth of vision, like the two eyes of the hunting owl. Or we will try to listen to sounds from two sources in such a way that they are stereophonic rather than conflicting noises. Or we will aim to be aware of both our movements and the music around us so that we can move in a dance, which is a picture of wisdom.

We could think about this in yet another way.

It is notable that in many Western churches it is not possible to see in from the outside, nor to see out when one is on the inside. Even if the windows are not of stained glass they are usually high, allowing only a distorted image of a patch of sky or of surrounding buildings, and they do not open. This could perhaps be symbolic of much Christian thinking. The aim of this book is to try to make some holes in the walls so that air can circulate, and so that people can see and move in and out more easily. We will begin by looking at the process of learning.

Chapter Two

Knowledge, Skill and Wisdom

Overview

Learning: Four Activities

Mention learning and most of us probably think of school. We will start there.

In a primary school classroom a child is looking out of the window. Two others are planning a game for play time. Another two are arguing over the ownership of a ruler. There are displays on the wall, and there is also a teacher. It is a hive of activity where learning is taking place.

The project is the Romans; they are learning about Roman roads, villas, and heating systems. There are some words on the wall in Latin and a photo of a mosaic of a Roman goddess, and another of a Roman altar. Some children are writing, others are drawing and several are talking about how they could make a video of a gladiator fight. The teacher stands up and calls for quiet, then points out that there is too much noise coming from the gladiator directors for others to be able to work properly. For a while the work continues quietly, then the sound begins to rise again.

Clearly in this classroom they are getting information about the Romans, and at least some of them are making some sense of it in their own minds. They might be making a mental comparison with their own life experience, or with that of the cavemen they did last term. One aim of the work in the class is for the children to make sense of what they are hearing, seeing, reading or being told: for them to acquire knowledge. This is the kind of activity in which Galileo was engaged. He had his information about the movements of the planets, the sun and the moon and, at some crucial point, a magnified view of the moon. In the process of making sense of this information he came to endorse Copernicus' theory about the solar system.

But that is not all that is going on. As they write their material and draw their diagrams the children are developing these skills. It may be that they are also acquiring some of the skills of the historical researcher: learning how to find information in reference sources and how to compare dates and designs. They may learn about how historians work, as well as how the Romans built their roads. Whilst they are making sense of information and acquiring knowledge they are also developing the skills of writing, reading, listening, drawing, handling technical equipment and carrying out research.

Galileo's technical skills were also considerable. He could not only read, write and argue, but he could construct his own telescope. Newton too was not only extremely skilled in mathematics at an early age but was able to set up his own equipment for experiments.

However, when the teacher points out that the enthusiastic noise of one group is causing problems for another, there is a brief change of focus for the classroom's activity, and a third kind of learning is taking place. Another feature of life in the classroom is that the children learn to live together. In a secondary school there might be an item on the timetable labelled 'social education' where this kind of thing is deliberately discussed, but from day one in a child's school life the child is learning to live with and work with others.

There may come occasions when the children begin to explore the whole business of Roman life from a fourth angle. While one group plan an action video of a gladiator fight, another might write a poem on the feelings of a gladiator before a contest, or after killing someone in a fight. The whole class might talk about why the Romans might have believed in many gods, and whether that made sense and, if someone was going to believe in many gods today, what they might be. They might think about whether having slaves was good or bad. Perhaps some would talk and write about their own thoughts after handling Roman coins which had actually been used by people nearly two thousand years ago. Here they are moving into another whole area. It is not about ordering information, nor skill development, nor about how people get on with each other, although it is related to all of those. It is an activity which might be called the gathering of wisdom.

Wisdom is about the value of things, about proportion and significance, about what might really matter, and one's place in the world and in time. The word has tended to drop out of use in the English language within the last century, although many ancient societies valued wisdom and sought it. The lack of use of the word may be an indication of the technological domination of Western society, in which people are much more comfortable dealing with things which can be measured, ordered and compared, than things which many feel to be vague and woolly. However, within the last three decades there has been a widespread questioning of the values behind the Western technological enterprise, and this could be seen as a search for wisdom.

These different kinds of learning are obviously not confined to the classroom. From birth a child develops skills and begins to make some sense of its experience of life. The child learns to control muscles, to distinguish between itself and its mother, to recognize sounds, and to make them. The process goes on through schooling, and continues in life. People in their forties have to learn new skills for work, and in their seventies often have to learn how to manage without the mobility they had when they were younger.

Everyone is always receiving new information about the world, whether it be football results, local news or the details of a new video. And in every new situation people have to work out how to get on with others, or to ignore them if that is what they choose to do. What happens is that these different activities come to the fore in different situations and at different times. The others do not stop, they simply move into a secondary position for a while.

On a training course the focus might be skill development, but during the tea break the primary task for participants will be establishing relationships, getting on with the others, and making connections.

The factory or workshop could be seen as the place where the primary focus is on the use and development of skills, although relationships between people and the sorting out of new information are still in evidence.

In the family a significant focus is more likely to be the bonding, building, and establishing of relationships, or trying to repair them, although the family home is also going to be a place where skills are developed and used.

The development of wisdom may likewise go on in any context, or it may be neglected. Perhaps religious centres like churches, synagogues and temples are the places one might expect this to come to the fore, although any place where people ask significant questions about their own lives and the world, or where they develop a sense of their own place within it and to appreciate what they are a part of, would be a place where wisdom might be acquired.

Changing Priorities

These different kinds of learning have a different emphasis in different cultures and different periods of history. The Romans are renowned for their technological development. It took a thousand years after the collapse of the Roman Empire for some of the Romans' organizational and technical skills to be redeveloped. But in many ways they were not very good at living together. The life of the cities was often violent and riots were frequent. The whole empire maintained a so-called peace through the harsh imposition of penalties and the military suppression of rebellions. It was said of the Romans, in Tacitus' *Agricola*: 'They make a desert and call it peace.'

Many Greeks, on the other hand, were not so interested in technology as in understanding and wisdom. And the Hebrews, at the time they were producing their Scriptures, placed a great importance on wisdom and appropriate relationships rather than on the speculative philosophy which developed in Greece.

In nineteenth-century Britain there was a great interest in technology, with a corresponding development of the manufacturing industry, but the religious interest of the time was largely seen as a form of social cement and stabilizer. In the 1960s there was an encouragement of technology and science amongst those who made policy decisions about education, whilst a counter-culture grew which questioned the accepted values and wanted new and more peaceful and creative ways for people to be able to live together.

As the emphasis shifts and varies from culture to culture, skills and insights are lost. This was true of the technical achievement of the Romans and of others. Some of the jewellery of the ancient Celts of Britain and Ireland has remarkable detail. No-one knows how it was done with the tools that were available at the time. It is not known how the great terracotta statues of China were actually made — how clay figures that size were fired without cracking. From Easter Island to Stonehenge the world is littered with technological puzzles.

The advance of Western culture into Africa and South America from the sixteenth century onwards led to the destruction of social relationships and, in places, these have not yet recovered. Social systems of tribes and nations were destroyed by the conquerors, and new ones are sometimes fragile or unstable.

Even without the wholesale destruction of societies by violent invasion, it is still the case that harmonious relationships can descend into violence and terror in the course of time. The skills of peaceful living are often lost. A new generation does not learn what is needed, or the organization cannot adjust to changed circumstances. What this means is that any society, whatever its achievements in some areas, could have something to learn from the people of another culture. It is possible that a society with great achievements in some areas is weak in others, and so could learn from another society, even one of another time. On that basis alone the writings, art, and insights of another culture could have value to the people of Western society.

The possibility of learning from other cultures is often recognized, even though it may not always be openly admitted. Many people in England want children at school to be taught Shakespeare though

Shakespeare actually belonged to a very different society from that which now exists in England. The industrialization and urbanization of the eighteenth and nineteenth centuries have changed English society into something quite different from that which William Shakespeare belonged to. Though they might not put it this way, anyone who wants a child to study Shakespeare for any other reason than to learn to quote famous lines, is hoping that the child can learn something from a very different kind of society.

This is openly declared by those who look to pre-Christian European religions, Tibetan Buddhism, Japanese Zen, or North American native teachings to give insight into the problems of life at the turn of the millennium. These people are often saying that Western society has 'dug itself into a hole'. It has developed great technological skills and complicated social organization but is causing damage to the life of the planet which it does not have the capacity to repair. Neither, they say, does Western society have the ability to develop harmonious relationships with the rest of humanity, let alone with the whole of the living planet. So they look to other societies for the skills and wisdom they believe are needed.

Principles, Pictures and Proverbs

In the development of skills and the acquisition of wisdom, as in other forms of learning, key images play a part. During one day, classroom teachers will use a whole array of different techniques to try and help the children in the classes to learn. They will get the children to read, draw, write, talk, and perhaps to act something out. On occasions they will show things to groups or individuals, perhaps in response to questions, or as a result of things they have noticed. This may be because they want the children to see something which will help them make some sense of order or pattern out of what they are finding out. Or it may be so that the children can see how something is done, and so be better able to do it themselves.

The teachers will ask questions. Some of these questions may send the children off to other sources of information to find things out for themselves. Some of the questions may be ones for them to mull over. Some of them may be questions which have no simple factual answer but call forth imagination or emotion. A teacher is not likely to analyse in detail the techniques being used. There is not time for that, and with a skilled teacher the different techniques have become second nature. What would be seen by an analyst is that different techniques are used according to the type of learning the teacher wants the child to experience.

The techniques for helping people order information and acquire understanding are different from those which help a person develop a skill. Similarly, when the focus is on the way that the class of children are getting on with each other, questions and rules may be used in a different way again. And when it is the development of wisdom that is the concern, imagination and exploratory thinking will be encouraged. Then there may be questions, pictures, drama, poems and storytelling.

The different types of learning have different forms, but they all employ key images in one way or another. We have already considered their use in the development of understanding: the organization of information into ordered patterns. We took the work of Galileo and Newton as examples of this.

In science there are significant models, or paradigms — theoretical constructs which provide a focus for a whole area of study. Flowers take a multitude of different forms. In order to make sense of this diversity a book on flowers might present in its introduction an example of an imaginary flower which has all the basic elements — the stem, sepal, petals, stamen, and so on. The individual flowers are then thought of as variations of this model.

Matter exists in three states — solids, liquids and gases. Some matter actually becomes gaseous from the solid state, but this is seen as an exception to a general pattern. The French language dictionary does not describe every form of every verb but lists an example of each of the regular verbs. It then gives details of the ones which are so exceptional that they cannot be described as being variations from this paradigm.

The learning of skills has less place for key images as it is an activity which largely involves the practice of co-ordinating body movement with the imagination and perception. But here there will be sayings or principles which the apprentice should note. The driving instructor tells the trainee, 'Mirror, signal, manoeuvre' until the learner driver automatically looks in the rear mirror and signals before moving position on the road. The carpenter tells the apprentice to cut beside the line for an accurate cut in a piece of wood. The music teacher has basic principles for posture and breathing, as well as the reading of the score. The example of the accomplished craftsman or artist may also provide a key image for others of how the skill can be employed.

In living together the learning or development of moral principles plays a part. These vary from points of etiquette, like how to address a stranger or someone in a position of influence, to significant practices like telling the truth or respecting other people's property. There may be occasions when it is appropriate not to keep to the principle. There may be times when it is good not to tell the truth or to speak when spoken to, but these are deviations from the norm. Some societies are strong on rules; others will employ principles.

In Hebrew society there developed a whole body of instruction on how people should live, which came to be known as the Torah, or Law. It had at its heart the Ten Commandments, though by the time of Jesus even that statement had come to be summarized in the brief instruction known as the *Shema*: 'You shall love the Lord your God with all your heart, soul, mind and strength; and your neighbour as yourself' (*Luke 10.25–28*). Alongside this there was also a great body of proverbial instruction, much of which, like the Torah, came to be gathered into the Bible. These proverbs were easily remembered sayings, some of which the student would hold fast to, and others which he might remember but seldom think about.

> *A soft answer turns away wrath,*
> *but a harsh word stirs up anger.*
> *Better is a dinner of vegetables where love is*
> *than a fatted ox and hatred with it.*
> *Those who are hot tempered stir up strife,*
> *but those who are slow to anger calm contention.*
>
> Proverbs 15.1, 17, 18

Proverbs are widespread throughout human society, giving pointers or guidelines for how people should live. Also common are stories, which may be of the simple 'moral tale' variety: so-and-so did such-and-such and look what happened to them. Or they might be much more cryptic and parabolic, the kind of thing that can roll around in the hearers imaginations and make them think over what is happening, what they are doing, and how they might be. Teachers of wisdom might employ many of these techniques. Those who acquire wisdom may have in their minds cryptic sayings or blunt proverbs, visual images or stories.

> *A neighbour came to borrow Nasrudin's donkey.*
> *'It's out on loan,' said Nasrudin.*
> *At that moment the animal began to bray from within the stable.*

'But I can hear it bray,' said the neighbour.
'So whom are you going to believe, the donkey or me?' [1]

Hebrew Insight

The ancient Hebrews were not particularly interested in what we might call knowledge or understanding. They did not spend a lot of time and energy gathering information about the world and putting it into some kind of clear pattern or logical order. Neither were they particularly technically-minded people. They developed no science and made no technological breakthroughs. However, their technology did change as time went on, as did their understanding of the world, and in the second and third centuries BC some Jews were engaged in the scientific and philosophical activity of their host cities. But this was in response to the initiatives and cultural developments of others. What did concern the Hebrews were questions of their place in the world, and how they should live together and with other people.

The Hebrews emerge in world history at about 1200 BC as a collection of small tribes settled in the southeast corner of the Mediterranean basin. They lived alongside other tribes as small farmers in a loose-knit organization. What was distinctive about them was their sense of identity. They had come, they believed, from Egypt, rescued from slavery by their god, Yahweh. They believed they were descended from a common ancestor, Abraham, and had been led to this place and given this land.

Two hundred years later they had cohered into two groups, thought of as ten northern tribes and two southern ones, but for a short while they had one king. Under David and his son, Solomon, they became a significant power in the Middle East. Then the kingdom split, and the two resulting kingdoms became very minor powers in the region.

The two kingdoms were continually at odds with each other, and three hundred years later the people of the north, the kingdom of Israel, were overrun and many were deported by their Assyrian conquerors. Then the southern kingdom, known as Judah, was destroyed by the Babylonian Empire. Having been reduced to a very minor power in world politics these people now faded very much into the background. But during all this time very significant things were going on in terms of religious development.

When the Hebrews became a united kingdom under David there was sufficient stability and leisure for people to write things down. They wrote some of their songs and laws. During the reign of Solomon a temple was built in Jerusalem, and the religious cult developed from being a simple practice focused on a number of shrines, to being something elaborate and centralized. This would have encouraged more writing. But still, as with most peoples of the time, much of their cultural material remained linked to the spoken word — stories, songs and poems passed down generations; rituals, music and dances, taught by one person to another — and the rules of behaviour learnt by each new generation of lawyers, political leaders and parents.

Hebrew culture was not something static. It developed as time went on. Through the course of their history the Hebrews' understanding of their place in the world and of the concerns and activities of their god altered. Yahweh was not only the God who would look after his people, but was one who was concerned for justice. He was concerned for those who had little power as well as the socially important and powerful. Yahweh not only had the ability to give victory in battle, or withhold it, but had influence over the weather and the crops. Yahweh was not one who could be cajoled into doing what people wanted, but took his own initiatives and had his own purposes. Yahweh was not only one who had brought the people into this land but had formed humanity from the earth in the first place.

The origin of the name, Yahweh, is obscure, but it seems to be connected with the Hebrew verb, 'to be'. In the Book of Exodus there is a story of Yahweh appearing to Moses in a bush which is burning, but is not burnt up (*Exodus 3*). Yahweh tells Moses to go to Egypt to lead the Israelites out of slavery, and Moses does not want to go so he thinks up a number of excuses. One is that he will need to be able to tell the Israelites God's name, and God says to him something which is usually translated as 'I am who I am'. This is the word pronounced in Hebrew something like 'Yahweh'. Except that in Hebrew it came to be unspoken. Out of reverence for the name of God when the letters of the Hebrew name were written in the text another word was said instead: the word '*Adonai*', which translates as 'Lord'. In many English translations of the Bible the word is translated as 'LORD'.

When Jerusalem was overrun by the Babylonians, the temple was destroyed and the leaders of the people were taken into exile. This was not only a political crisis, but a cultural and theological crisis as well. In exile the storytellers and scribes worked to make sense of what had happened, re-telling the story of their people. The priests wrote down much of what they had remembered, and developed that, together with a vision of what a new temple and its worship could be.

At the same time, new teachers and preachers opened out the religious insight of the people into new dimensions, providing a new vision of the world. The work of these preachers, or prophets, is contained, among other places, in the opening of the book of Genesis and the later sections of the book of Isaiah.

These prophets' vision was that Yahweh was not only the God of the Hebrews, he was the one God. Yahweh had not only formed humanity from the earth but had called the world into being at the beginning of all things. Yahweh was not only powerful but was able to work through the weak and the oppressed. Sometimes being true to Yahweh would lead to suffering and grief. But Yahweh had not only taken decisive action in the past, he would do so again in the future. Despite the destruction of the temple and this exile of the people, Yahweh could still be trusted.

The Origin of the Bible

The Babylonian Empire was taken over by the Persians, and some of the leading Hebrews returned to Jerusalem. For some of them their dream was to rebuild the city and the great temple, and slowly some work was done on this, but life had changed. The majority of Hebrews continued to live outside Palestine. They were known as the Diaspora, or Dispersion. They tended now to be known not so much as Hebrews, but as Jews, a name developed from the name of the dominant tribe of the old southern kingdom: Judah. In the dispersion they spoke freely and wrote in the language of their host country.

Though the temple in Jerusalem remained important, religious life was no longer focused so much on the central temple as on the books and the meeting house. The meeting house took its Greek name, the synagogue. Within the synagogue one could study the sacred books. The key people in the cultural life were now the teachers, or rabbis. They interpreted the books and memorized and passed on previous interpretations and judgements. In due course these interpretations came to be collected together as the Talmud.

After the Jewish leaders were able to return to Jerusalem there were six centuries when the Jewish people in Palestine were ruled as a client kingdom or simply a province of successive Persian, Greek and Roman Empires. There was one short period after a particularly bloody war, when they had a measure of independence under their own Hasmonean kings, but it did not last long. The Jews of Palestine were a subject people, but with dreams of freedom.

By the time the Romans had control of Palestine there was as yet no Bible but several collections of writings. Firstly there was the Torah: the Instruction, or Law. Then there were the Books of the Prophets, and there were the Writings. Then there were other books, circulated amongst various groups and factions, containing rules for their groups, visions of hope or disaster, pithy sayings, stories, poems, and much more. All Jews accepted the Law as of prime importance. After that there was disagreement; Jewish society was not united. Some saw the Prophets and the Writings as of great value, as Scriptures given by God. Others valued them less. Amongst the multitude of other books, there were a variety of opinions. There was also argument and in-fighting over other matters, including a severe difference of opinion over how to respond to the rule of the pagan Romans, and over what Yahweh God might be doing about it all. After the Roman occupation of Palestine there was a century of religious, cultural and political turmoil, and a reshaping of the map for Jews and non-Jews alike.

Looked at from our vantage point, three significant features of this can be noted.

First, for a century or so, there had been movements looking for, or claiming to have, a messiah. The Messiah was literally God's King — one who would bring in the rule of God. Alleged messiahs were successively put down by the Roman rulers.

During the rule of Herod Antipas in Galilee and Pontius Pilate in Judea there was a messianic movement focused on a seemingly self-taught rabbi called Jesus, from Nazareth. He was executed by Pilate with the collusion of the Jewish authorities, but his followers did not disperse and disappear. They continued to preach, to teach and to carry out healings in much the same way Jesus had, and the movement grew rapidly. They claimed Jesus had risen from the dead and continued to be at work.

In time the movement took in not only Jews but non-Jews, or Gentiles as they were called, and within fifty years it had become a significant religious movement within the Roman Empire and beyond. People involved in this movement came to be called Christians — *christos* being the Greek translation of the Hebrew word *messiah*.

Secondly, forty years after Jesus' execution, there was a large and violent rebellion against Roman rule which resulted in the destruction of the temple and the deaths of thousands of Jewish rebels. Fifty years after that another rebellion, this one with another alleged messiah at its head, was put down by the Romans, and access to Jerusalem was forbidden to Jews.

Thirdly, in response to the crises produced by the destruction of the temple and the growing Christian movement, Jewish leaders met at Jamnia and drew up a definitive list of holy books, including the Law, the Prophets and the Writings. The Christians generally accepted this collection as their own scriptures, with the addition of a still growing smaller collection of their own writings, principally books about Jesus and letters from leaders to Christian groups.

In time the Christian collection settled to being a more or less fixed set of books and there emerged what Christians came to call the Bible. It contained the Jewish Scriptures, known to Christians as the books of the Old Testament, and the Christian writings which they called the books of the New Testament. There were also books which were not included in the Old Testament, and did not belong in the New, but were often read and treated with respect. They were generally known as the Apocrypha, and are included today in many Bibles either among the Old Testament books or as a third section.

Jews and Christians continued to produce books. The Talmud came to be written down by Jewish rabbis. There were writings by leading Christians, and other books about Jesus emerged from the various religious movements in Europe and the Middle East in the centuries following the council of Jamnia. These books about Jesus tend to be called Apocryphal Gospels. They are called gospels because, like the ones in the New Testament, they purport to tell the good news of Jesus. *Godspel* is Old English for good news. They are called apocryphal because they often claim to tell of things taught by Jesus in secret; the word apocryphal coming from the Greek words –*apos*, from, and *kryptein*, hidden.

The Bible and Learning

Pick up a Bible and what you have in your hand is a translation of some of the world's oldest books. Some of the psalms, laws and stories in the Bible were written down three thousand years ago, about the same time as the oldest Hindu scriptures, the *Rig Veda*. Other parts of the Bible were written in the centuries following, often after many generations of being handed down by word of mouth: as songs or rules which had to be remembered verbatim; in the context of acts of worship where a verse or response might be altered or added; as tales told to show the significance of what was happening in the world; or as pure entertainment. Much of the Old Testament had a long history of retelling or even rewriting before it reached the form it has now, which it only acquired shortly before the time of Jesus.

In the New Testament there are four gospels, written between thirty and fifty years after Jesus' work in Galilee and Jerusalem. These largely contain material which had been used in those decades in preaching and teaching. They focus on Jesus — what he said, what he did, and what happened to him.

The gospels have two levels of significance. Firstly, each book is the result of one particular writer's interest and work. The writers were not working in isolation but were members of a community, and shared the concerns and interests of that group. Each writer would have gathered material from others. He may have drawn on their own memories, going back to the time of Jesus which was only thirty years or so before. The writer may have had another book or two in front of him when he came to write. But each writer would have had his own concerns and emphases, and written to try to get a message across. At one level we are reading that message, and are in a position to gain something from that person's insight.

On a second level there is the person of Jesus himself. Behind the gospels is this man — his teaching and his life. Sometimes it is possible to see quite clearly what that was. At other times the different angles of the different gospel writers make it hard to see exactly what actually happened back there in Galilee and Judea. That means that if we are engaged in a historical search for the teachings or life of the man, Jesus, we are often stuck for a detailed answer. Sometimes we can work out the detail. At other times, though we have a strong sense of a person of unique insight and impressive personality behind this book, the detail of what he said and did is elusive.

This means that while reading the gospels it is sometimes possible to get close to what was actually done by and to this person, Jesus of Nazareth. At other times we cannot do that, but we do have the insight of someone who was in the first generation of his disciples. For someone who reckons that Jesus is worth taking seriously, the writings of those close to him in time and in understanding are going to be of immense value.

Also within the New Testament is a book telling of the first years of the Christian movement, the Acts of the Apostles. This is similar in style to the gospels, and is clearly intended as a sequel to one of them, written by the same person. As there is only one such book there is no possibility of comparing what this one says with other accounts of the emergence of the early Church. As with the gospels, even if one considers one is not reading historical detail, one can still gain from reading what someone who was caught up in the whole thing has to say. As with many other books in the Bible, it is not only an account of untrammelled success. There are failures, mistakes and disagreements documented here as well.

The New Testament also has a collection of letters by early leaders of that movement. These too give a glimpse of communities struggling through argument and crisis to live in accord with the way of Jesus. They are letters which were written to address particular issues in specific churches, but have been treated by churches since then as giving helpful instruction and insight which can have a bearing on many other situations as well.

The collection ends with a book of fantastic visions by a church leader during one of the first periods of persecution, known as the Book of Revelation. Like the letters, it addresses particular situations but has continued to be valued by churches since that time. In some Christian groups it has been highly prized. Its obliqueness and complexity has enabled people to treat it as a quarry for the construction of any number of further fantasies and idiosyncratic theories.

Bearing in mind the cultural emphases of the Hebrew and Jewish people, their concerns and their history, we can expect to find no science and little philosophy in the Bible. Their telling of their story will not be a secular history. It will not be an ordering of the information to give a picture of how past events would have been experienced by the people, or how the activities in one place fitted in with regional or global movements and events. It will be an ordering of collected stories retold to present a view of what Yahweh God was doing in the past, and to explain how and why God had brought about the present situation or allowed it to happen.

We can also expect little in the Bible that is to do with the transmission of skills and technology. The writers were not great technical innovators and what technical skill was passed on in any societies was rarely committed to writing by anyone anywhere before the last few centuries, let alone by the ancient Hebrews. What we can expect in the Bible is a whole array of material of different kinds concerned with how people are to live together. Much of this will be very local, concerned with them as a people and relevant to their time. However they were concerned not only with their relationships with each other and with the land, but also with Yahweh, whom they came to see as the only God, the ultimate locus of creative power and justice. Though located in a particular time and society this could therefore have some relevance for any society.

There will also be much in the Bible which is concerned with wisdom, the whole matter of the place and significance of people and of the world, of what is and what is not really important.

It is on this basis that we will be looking at the Bible in the next chapters. We will not be expecting the Bible to present us with scientific models to make sense of the information available to us in our own age, nor to provide us with an understanding of the way our minds develop and work. We will be looking to see how the insights of the biblical writers relate to some of our own ways of viewing the world, and of understanding ourselves. We will also be seeing what they might say about how we can live together on this planet freely, creatively, wisely, and with enjoyment and humour.

1   Anthony de Mello, *The Heart of the Enlightened* (Fount, London, 1989) p. 69

Chapter Three

The Planet and the Cosmos

Overview

Cycles of Life

One of the things I like to do if I have a period of free time is to go walking. If I can walk near the coast that is a real bonus. I prefer not to walk on the well worn paths but to find my own way between places, and this involves using a map quite extensively. By the time I stop somewhere for lunch I am likely to have looked at the Ordnance Survey map of the area a number of times.

Pubs near the coast often decorate their walls with sea charts. Not being a sailor, these do not mean a great deal to me, but I do find the difference between the sea chart and the Ordnance Survey map of the coastal area interesting. What is of great importance to the sailor matters very little to the walker, but the person in the boat is not concerned with bridges over streams, telephone boxes and bridle-paths. A land map and a sea chart of a piece of coastline can look quite different, though they are maps of one and the same place.

Walking along the coast one occasionally notices pipelines heading out to sea. These are often sewer pipes from a coastal village or town. This is the local community getting rid of its waste. But to the things that live in the sea this is something just arriving, which may not be welcome. A flock of gulls hovering round the end of a sewer outfall are clearly pleased with some of what is coming out. But the mental separation of land and sea has led industrialized society to pour tons of material into the sea which will not break down into matter which can be ingested by marine life, but will cause disease and death to living organisms. The North Sea particularly is one of the most polluted in the world, with an accumulation of waste from Britain and Northern Europe.

The same kind of thing happens with other waste. Where I live, our rubbish is collected once a week. We put it into plastic bags and leave it by the gate, then a lorry comes and takes it away. We may have got rid of it, but it has only been removed from our own little area. It has now arrived somewhere else, probably a big hole in the ground.

Sometimes if I have garden rubbish to get rid of I burn it. That way it does not fill up the landfill site used by the council, but the material does not disappear. The wood becomes smoke, ash and gases. The smoke and ash go into the air. The smoke finally falls somewhere else, on a near neighbour's land or further away, carried by the moving air, and perhaps brought down by the rain.

Matter moves around and changes its form. Salts in the soil are built up with carbon from the air into plant cells. These cells may be burnt, releasing the chemicals into the air or returning some to the soil. The gases in the air may be rebuilt by a later generation of plants, or return to the soil in rainwater. Some of the plants may be eaten, and become part of the cells of animals or insects. In turn these die and the matter returns to the soil. Some matter is changed by people into metal, stone, wood or plastic structures. In turn these slowly return to the ground, though in the case of some of these materials it is an extremely slow process for them to become anything other than solid blocks of material.

Though we tend to see the world as separate entities — the sea and the land, my garden and my neighbour's, the tractor and the field, the cows and the grass, the road, the cars and the pedestrians — these are actually all a part of one whole.

Anyone reading this will be breathing. The air enters our lungs; some of the oxygen within it is absorbed by our red blood cells and carried to the different muscles and organs of our body. It was a part of the air but now the oxygen is a part of us. In time we breathe it out, combined with carbon. This carbon dioxide may then be absorbed by a plant and become a part of the plant's cell structure. Another person may in turn eat the plant, and some of the plant material becomes a part of their body.

So it goes on. This is something which Western society is slowly becoming more aware of, and the key image of this insight is the circle. Biology has in the last few decades become less interested in the lives of animals and plants, and more interested in the ecological cycles: how one is related to another. People are now deliberately recycling materials, and people in Europe and North America are increasingly aware that what is done to the rainforests in the south or the seas in the north affects everyone.

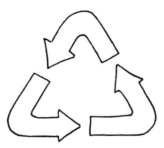

This is not a new insight, but it is something which was forgotten in Europe and North America, and is having to be re-learnt. Indian, Celtic and earlier North American societies had a sense of the interconnectedness of life, but European society lost it and has carried out immense industrial enterprise without thinking of the consequences. Trees were removed without replanting. Waste went into the air and the sea and poisons were sprayed on the soil. Then people started dying in the smog, and the birds began to disappear from the countryside. The fish and the seals were diseased, and slowly people began to realize what was happening.

Perhaps that is the scenario. At this point in history it is hard to say whether enough people have begun to realize what is happening for the damage to be limited or repaired. But the interconnectedness of all life and matter is a growing awareness within Western society.

Time and Change

Most people in Britain can remember changes in the world around them: the supermarket changed its name or the people who worked there had a different style of overall; the bus timetable was altered; a new road was built; some trees were cut down; or a new hedge was planted. This is a feature of life, and of the landscape. There are cuttings and roads where once there were fields; quarries in the sides of hills have been made bigger. New woods have been planted and farmland has been made into housing estates. But even before people started altering the landscape it was happening anyway. The change has generally been very slow and continuous.

Where a new road is being built the ground is cut away and the first layer is turf and rich soil. Looked at closely it is seen to contain fibres and granules; there might be minute insects or an earthworm. Below that, the soil changes colour becoming more granular and lifeless. Below this subsoil there is possibly broken rock, and below that the cutting may even have been into solid rock. The layer of topsoil is not deep, perhaps half a metre at the most. This is the part in which food is grown, and there is not much of it. In hilly countryside the land rolls on, with fields of cattle, or crops, marked out by hedges and woodland. But the soil in which all this grows is thin. It is a mere skim over the top of sterile rock, and it has taken a long time to form.

Fifteen thousand years ago in Britain there was little soil. The north was covered in ice, or severely scoured by glaciers. The south was tundra — very cold with mosses, lichens and some small shrubs and grasses struggling to take hold. When the land warmed and the ice grew less, slowly the plant life increased until the land was largely covered by forests in which animals and humans moved. The topsoil today is largely the result of generations of trees and other plants turning the salts in the deeper rocks into leaf and branch, and then dying and becoming the humus of the soil.

The granules in the soil are made from rock which has been broken down by water and ice, frosts, rivers, glaciers, and by the action of roots. This formation of the clays and sands which form the bulk of the soil has also taken thousands of years, but has been going on in cycles for thousands of millennia. In the part of the country where I live, the underlying rock is limestone, so the bulk of the soil is formed from clays ground out of the solid limestone by centuries of water and ice.

The limestone was formed hundreds of thousands of years ago, at the bottom of the sea. Small living organisms fell to the ocean floor and their calcium rich cells formed a thick layer of sediment. Then with the slow movement of the earth's crust these were buried below other matter and compressed. Slowly they surfaced again as solid limestone. Elsewhere in Britain there are sandstones, formed of compressed granules which had previously been ground away from other earlier rocks.

This is the way the planet is — continually, slowly changing. The rocks at the top of Mount Everest are limestone, formed below the ocean. The much smaller Grampian mountains of Scotland are older than the Alps and the Himalayas, but have been ground down to mere stumps by hundreds of millennia of wind, rain and ice, whilst other mountains have been raised up by the slow movement of the continental plates of the earth's surface.

The planet itself formed way back — a cooling, mass of rock, spinning around the sun. Slowly life formed on it which initially consisted of simple living cells, but very slowly more complicated organisms developed, and eventually mammals, and at some point there evolved humanity. Along the way millions of species have come and gone: some large and noticeable, like dinosaurs and mammoths, others lost into the limestones, chalks and mudstones of the planet, gone without trace of their existence as a species, let alone as individuals. Humanity has come lately on the scene, and within only a few centuries humanity has drastically altered the appearance of the earth's surface.

In ancient Jericho there is a tower. It is circular and can only be seen from the top because the layers of debris of centuries have piled up around it. The tower is ten thousand years old; it was built when the forests were slowly establishing themselves when the ice receded in Britain. Within the whole age of the planet that is a mere slither of time. But that seems to be us — humanity — a species having developed within the last few moments of a very long process of change on the planet.

Open Space

When Galileo turned his telescope on the night sky he saw stars no-one had ever seen before, and he still saw only a small fraction of what is now known to be there. On a clear night the sky can seem ablaze with stars, most of which are larger than our own sun. Some of these stars, which appear to be single points of light, when magnified a hundred times can be seen to be clusters of stars, or whole galaxies. Some are large and old, others are small and relatively young, and all are moving.

For thousands of years humans have looked at the sky and marvelled. To them it seemed consistent and regular, an unchanging pattern moving through the year in a great sweep of darkness and light. Only the planets moved in their different courses across the night sky. Copernicus put the sun at the centre and visualized the planets moving around it, and by the time Kepler had done his calculations the course of the solar system seemed a simple regular pattern. The patterns of the planets was also a part of one consistent harmonic movement.

But more powerful instruments revealed that all was not as it seemed to the naked eye, and new maps were drawn. Now the solar system is drawn as one small part of one galaxy among many sweeping out into open space, moving like the debris of a great explosion. Billions of years ago, that is what it was: a great explosion, the big bang. But the explosion continues. The debris has not settled. It continues to move, ever outwards, with energy flowing through it, suns exploding and collapsing, and planets spinning around them, spiralling out and returning inwards. And on one such planet is you, reading this book.

This is the world we live in – a small planet, orbiting a small star, in the outer reaches of an expanding universe. But on that planet there is life, and at least one of those life forms has imagination, creativity, the ability to develop and use tools, to think, learn, reflect, be aware of the world, and to make and read books. Most of the time we do not think about that. We think about the next meal, the television programme, where we will go for a holiday and how we are going to pay the mortgage. But if we stop and think about it, that, we will say, is what the world is like.

The Hebrew View of the World

The people who wrote the Bible did not think about it like that. To them the world was basically flat, and over it stretched the dome of sky. Each morning the sun rose, and in the evening it went down again, having ridden across the sky in a smooth path. At night one might see the moon, tracing a similar path across the dome, or firmament. One would also usually see stars, moving in their seasonal cycle in a beautiful, restful pattern.

During the day one worked, except on the Sabbath. During the night if it was cold one could look at the fire. If it was warm one could look at the sky. One could talk, tell stories, sing songs, and go to bed — a simple life really. All one had to worry about was the blight, the locusts, the Assyrians, the moneylenders, thieves, disease, arthritis, drought, what one's neighbours thought, and numerous nameless things which seemed to make life troublesome or downright dangerous.

It was a simple life in many ways, but not an easy one. Still, many of them had time and the ability to think, and they took time to pray. When they came to write their books they came up with a number of interesting perspectives on the world which they knew themselves to be a part of.

• *A world full of marvels*

To the Hebrews the world was awesome and marvellous. They were not inclined to wax lyrical about the beauty of the world, and perhaps valued human companionship more highly than beautiful scenery, but they were not unaware of the power, mystery and beauty of the world. The mountains of the north, and the cedars of Lebanon, were bywords for beauty. The writer of Psalm 104 marvelled at the life of the world, and praised God for it:

> *O Lord my God, you are very great.*
> *You are clothed with honour and majesty,*
> *wrapped in light as with a garment.*
> *You make springs gush forth in the valleys;*
> *they flow between the hills,*
> *giving drink to every wild animal;*
> *the wild asses quench their thirst.*
> *By the streams the birds of the air have their habitation;*
> *they sing among the branches.*
>
> *(Psalm 104. 1, 10–12)*

• *The breath of life*

A part of this whole marvel was life itself, which was brought forth by God, and is somehow linked with the life of God. There is a Hebrew word, *ruach*, which is used to describe the wind and the breath of a person, and the life, or Spirit, of God. All these were *ruach*.

So the writer of the same psalm says:

> *These all look to you*
> *to give them their food in due season;*
> *when you give it to them, they gather it up;*
> *when you open your hand,*
> *they are filled with good things.*
> *When you hide your face they are dismayed;*
> *when you take away their breath they die*
> *and return to their dust.*
> *When you send forth your spirit (or breath),*
> *they are created;*
> *and you renew the face of the ground.*
>
> (Psalm 104.27–30)

In the second chapter of Genesis there is a story of the creation of humanity. It begins with the man being made from the ground:

> *In the day that the Lord God made the earth and*
> *the heavens, when no plant of the field was yet in*
> *the earth and no herb of the field had yet sprung up*
> *— for the Lord God had not yet caused it to rain*
> *upon the earth, and there was no one to till the*
> *ground, but a stream would rise from the ground*
> *and water the whole face of the ground — then the*
> *Lord God formed man from the dust of the ground,*
> *and breathed into his nostrils the breath of life; and*
> *the man became a living being.*
>
> (Genesis 2.4–7)

• The whole person

The man here becomes 'a living being'. He is a whole; he is not a body with a soul or animated dust. So Hebrews would talk or write about their heart, their bones, their stomach, or their kidneys as English writers might talk about their emotions. Life was lived in the body. The person was a living being, and injury done to the body was injury to the person. So joy was also experienced and expressed in the body.

Hebrews would also talk about the arm, the mouth or the hand of

God. The use of language about the body does not necessarily mean that God was thought of as having a corporeal existence. He was perhaps sometimes thought of as having these physical characteristics, but such talk was inevitable given the way that Hebrew thought and language worked. It was with the body that they experienced and did things so bodily language was inevitably transferred over to God.

Often English translations of the Bible use the word 'spirit' for the Hebrew *ruach*. Clearly as time went on God came to be thought of and spoken about in less human terms. The word *ruach* not only conjured up a vision of the wind moving through grass or of the breathing of a child, but of something more abstract, which was the essence of life. So it is that translators often choose the more abstract 'spirit' for the life essence of a person or of God.

• *Called into being by God*

The opening chapter of Genesis was written later, during the time of exile after the Babylonians had destroyed the temple in Jerusalem. Here God is described as calling a world into existence out of the waters. For the Hebrews the sea, which they feared as unpredictable, dangerous and changing, was symbolic of what the Greeks called *chaos*. Originally the world was formless and empty:

> *In the beginning when God created the heavens*
> *and the earth, the earth was a formless void*
> *and darkness covered the face of the deep, while*
> *a wind from God swept over the face of the waters.*
>
> *Then God said, 'Let there be light'; and there was*
> *light. And God saw that the light was good; and*
> *God separated the light from the darkness. God*
> *called the light Day, and the darkness he called*
> *Night. And there was evening*
> *and there was morning, the first day.*
>
> *(Genesis 1.1–5)*

First to be called from the chaos are time, light and darkness. Then there are further separations of sky and earth, land and seas, and then the world is filled with living creatures:

> *On the second day God called into being a dome*
> *to separate the waters, above and below.*

> *On the third day God called for the waters*
> *to be gathered together in one place, as seas,*
> *and for dry land to appear.*
> *And on the land*
> *God called for plants of differing kinds*
> *to come forth.*
> *On the fourth day God called for lights in the sky*
> *to be a sign for the seasons,*
> *and for the two great lights*
> *to rule the day and the night.*
> *On the fifth day God called into being*
> *the fish and sea monsters,*
> *and the birds of the air.*
> *On the sixth day God called forth animals*
> *and creeping things on the land.*
> *Each day as God called his creation into existence*
> *he saw that it was good.*
>
> *(Genesis 1.6–25, abridged)*

• *The image of God*

The next move in the whole drama comes after some deliberation:

> *Then God said, 'Let us make humankind in our*
> *image, according to our likeness; and let them have*
> *dominion over the fish in the sea, and over the birds*
> *of the air, and over the cattle, and over all the wild*
> *animals of the earth, and over every creeping thing*
> *that creeps upon the earth.'*
>
> *So God created humankind in his own image;*
> *in the image of God he created them;*
> *male and female he created them.*
>
> *(Genesis 1.26–27)*

Male and female humans are together made in 'the image of God'. There has been a great deal of argument over the meaning of this phrase, though it clearly belongs with the statement that follows. It is not the male who is the image of God, it is humanity of both sexes. And nothing else is specified — no skin colour, age, ability, or size.

• Power and responsibility

*God blessed them, and God said to them, 'Be fruit-
ful and multiply, fill the earth and subdue it; and
have dominion over the fish in the sea and over the
birds of the air and over every living thing that
moves upon the earth.'*

(Genesis 1.28)

In this poem, humans being 'the image of God' is linked with their having power over the other living things of the earth. This power was clearly limited, as everyone knew. Elsewhere, the writer of the Book of Job pointed this out forcefully when he has God ask Job whether he has tamed Leviathan, the great sea monster, or can do anything to make the rhinoceros obey him. Nevertheless humanity does have some power, which is seen by the writer as having been given by God. It is not a power that humanity has achieved by some prowess or virtue — it is given. And it is given by God the creator, not some malignant power. Humanity is to rule the living beings of the earth and, as 'the image of God', is to be God to them.

Originally, says the writer, this power and authority did not extend to eating the animals and fish. God gave plants to the humans and animals for food. In the whole book of Genesis the authority to eat meat only comes after Noah has rescued the animals and birds from the flood which God sent to wipe out humanity when he was fed up with humanity's violence.

• A whole world

Finally:

*God saw everything he had made, and
indeed, it was very good. And there was evening
and there was morning, the sixth day.*

*Thus the heavens and the earth were finished,
and their multitude. And on the seventh day God
finished the work he had done ...
and he blessed the seventh day and hallowed it,
because on it God rested from all the work
that he had done in creation.*

(Genesis 1.31–2.3)

The heavens and the earth were completed. Here there is a view of the world as being a whole; the world is now complete. If any of those components were removed there would be something missing. Though the birds and the animals, the sea monsters and the creeping things are all separate entities, they are still part of the whole. And so is humanity; human beings are also a part of that one world.

• *Cycles, patterns, labour and rest*

The pattern and the need for rest is repeated elsewhere. Again in Psalm 104:

> *When the sun rises the young lions withdraw*
> *and lie down in the dens.*
> *People go out to their work*
> *and to their labour until the evening.*
>
> *(Psalm 104.22–23)*

This is stated most clearly by the writer of Ecclesiastes:

> *For everything there is a season,*
> *and a time for every matter under heaven:*
> *a time to be born, and a time to die;*
> *a time to plant,*
> *and a time to pluck up what is planted;*
> *a time to kill, and a time to heal;*
> *a time to break down, and a time to build up;*
>
> *(Ecclesiastes 3.2–3)*

And so he continues with a picture of the cycles and rhythms of the world, and of its grief and joy.

• *The limitations of human understanding*

Humanity, though created in the image of God, is limited in ability and understanding. The book of Job contains the nearest thing in the Old Testament to a philosophical argument. The setting is that Job, though a thoroughly good man, has a thoroughly bad time. He argues with his friends who in various ways suggest that he must not be as good as he thinks, but he holds out in declaring that it is all unjust. In the end God speaks to him:

'Who is this that darkens counsel
by words without knowledge?
Gird up your loins like a man,
I will question you,
and you shall declare to me.
Where were you when I laid
the foundation of the earth?
Tell me, if you have understanding.
Who determined its measurements —
surely you know!

(Job 38.1–5)

And, line after line, God gets Job to look at the world around him and recognize its intricacy, power and mysteriousness, and in the end simply accept that there are things he does not know and cannot know, and to stop complaining.

Then Job answered the Lord:
'See I am of small account;
what shall I answer you?
I lay my hand on my mouth.'

(Job 40.4)

• *God has the prime wisdom*

Much of the world remains a mystery, but it is not chaotic. Psalm 104 says:

O Lord, how manifold are your works!
In wisdom you have made them all;
the earth is full of your creatures.
May the glory of the Lord endure forever;
may the Lord rejoice in his works.

(Psalm 104.24, 31)

It is created by the unfathomable wisdom of God. It shows God's power:

The heavens are telling the glory of God;
and the firmament proclaims his handiwork.
Day to day pours forth speech,
and night to night declares knowledge.

(Psalm 19.1–2)

• *God enjoys the world*

As in Psalm 104, so elsewhere the world is enjoyed by God, and may be enjoyed by humanity:

> *When I look at your heavens,*
> *the work of your fingers,*
> *the moon and the stars that you have established;*
> *what are human beings*
> *that you are mindful of them,*
> *mortals, that you care for them?*
> *Yet you have made him little lower than God,*
> *and crowned them with glory and honour.*
>
> *(Psalm 8.3–4)*

Compatible Views?

For the Hebrews the world was relatively small, and the earth was flat, though it was wonderful and mysterious. God was often spoken of in human and homely terms, but he was his own master, and not to be trifled with. The response of many writers reflecting on the visible vastness of the sky, the complex diversity of life, and the sheer power of the natural world, was one of awe at the creativity and majesty of God.

Our perception of the world is very different; we see ourselves on a planet in a vast universe. But on this rock sphere moving through infinite space there is a complex web of life within which we are bound, with all our potential and limitations — the result of billions of years of development and change. The whole framework in which we think about the world is different, though our response could be similar, and the Hebrew insights into the relationship of the world, humanity and God, are not incompatible with ours.

There are many things which would have caused a Hebrew to marvel but for which we have an explanation, or with which we are so familiar that we take them for granted. But even if the vastness of the cosmos and the intricacy of the whole system of life were not enough to rouse wonder within us, there would still be the possibility of marvelling that it exists at all.

The processes of life can now be described in some detail and, when breathing stops, life can for some time be maintained with sophisticated equipment. But the fact that a complex configuration of molecules can give rise to a form of existence which is on another plane, as a living being, can generate a sense of wonder. The fact that this developed in increasing complexity and gave rise to consciousness and awareness, could strike a person as positively awesome.

There seems to be an almost primeval reverence for life amongst humans. Though they remain in the news for only a short time, mass murders create a sense of shock and horror amongst people. Mass starvation may go on in parts of the world whilst the well-fed push it from their consciousness, but this often seems to be from a sense of helplessness or an inability to grasp the scale of what is happening, rather than because what is happening does not matter. In the complex and crowded world of the late twentieth century great resources are available for the destruction of large numbers of people, but this can only be spoken about with military euphemisms. There is no shortage of human life on the planet, yet considerable resources are spent to develop and employ technology to keep people alive.

It is as if people are here reacting unconsciously with a sense that other people have value. The outcry and unease about the extinction of species through human action is not only on the basis that these things might be useful to us, that there might be plants in the Amazon rainforest which could provide a cure for cancer. Many people seem to see the world as being valuable in itself. The Hebrew writers would have agreed with this, saying that it mattered because it was God's creation.

The complex web of life on this planet is now seen as having developed over a vast span of time, but that does not mean it cannot be seen as having been created. The greater understanding that we have of the complexity of the universe might perhaps reinforce the sense that it has come about purposefully; the more we know the more we can marvel at. The question arises as to how God was involved in the process, but that is not a new question. The ancient Hebrew could ask the same question. How did God move the sun and moon? How did he breathe life into the dying earth so that the life returned with the changing seasons? How was a child formed in the womb?

The Hebrews knew God was not to be seen at work, and in the great poem at the beginning of Genesis, God calls form, order and life into existence. It is as if the world comes into being in the mind of God, or as if God calls it out like a producer of a play. Yet the life or Spirit of God continues to work within it. One does not see the artist in the picture or hear the composer in the music, yet there is something of themselves within each. The world is an ever changing picture or a piece of extemporary music, and the Creator is continually at work within it.

Humanity has a place of significance within this creation. Humanity has power, but also responsibility. The power of humanity on the planet earth cannot be disputed. What the biblical writer couples with it is responsibility. Humanity, to be true to its nature, is to treat the world as its Creator treats it, to care as the Creator cares, and to enjoy it with the Creator. And this is not just for some part of humanity — the male part — or people of one particular race or of special ability. It is all humanity that is in the image of God.

This puts a challenge to Western society. The earth, with this view, is not simply a natural resource for its life forms to be used or destroyed to satisfy the desires of one part of humanity. The life of the planet has a value in its own right, as God's creation, and all humanity has importance as made in the image of God. And because humanity is endowed by God with power within the world people are responsible to God for how they use it.

The damage being done to life on the planet is becoming clear for all to see. A crippling difficulty is knowing what can be done about it. For the Hebrew the ultimate wisdom rested with God. Wisdom meant not so much acquiring information, as living with a sense of, and respect for, God and acting in accord with God's purposes. God's world was not one of relentless struggle, but of work and of rest. Those who harmonized with the ways of God would find the resources for the tasks they needed to undertake. The prophet Isaiah, addressing the demoralized Jews in their exile in Babylon, wrote:

> *The Lord is the everlasting God,*
> *the Creator of the ends of the earth.*
> *He does not faint or grow weary;*

> *his understanding is unsearchable.*
> *He gives power to the faint,*
> *and strengthens the powerless.*
>
> *Even youths will faint and be weary,*
> *and the young will fall exhausted;*
> *but those who wait for the Lord*
> *shall renew their strength,*
> *they shall mount up with wings like eagles,*
> *they shall run and not be weary,*
> *they shall walk and not faint.*
>
> *(Isaiah 40.28–31)*

Part of that waiting for Yahweh would be recognizing that the world is enjoyed by its Creator, and to be appreciated and enjoyed by humanity.

Real Wisdom?

The fact that this Hebrew way of seeing the world as God's creation is in some ways compatible with a twentieth-century view of life and the universe does not necessarily mean it is true. But how does one judge? Testing a new scientific theory one conducts experiments and uses mathematics and logic. But when assessing whether a piece of advice is good for relationships between people one tries to assess whether it makes sense in different ways. Does it fit in with one's understanding of the people concerned, and their needs and aspirations? Does it square with one's sense of justice?

Again, if someone comes out with a suggestion about how to do a particular piece of work one would try to anticipate whether it would work, and if not, why not? One might try it out and see the result. Here we are dealing with something that is not a scientific or historical theory. It is to do with relationships, and with the values which might lie behind one's decisions about what should or should not be done. We are also dealing here with wisdom, or with foolishness. The criteria for judging wisdom are less clear. Perhaps wisdom simply rings true, or it does not.

This view is not without its problems. There is the whole question of what we are talking about when we use the word 'God'. For some people the word may conjure up a vision of a great being somewhere within a part of the universe called 'heaven'. And that may be what many Hebrews had in mind when they spoke of Yahweh. Nevertheless that is clearly not what is meant here. 'The heavens and the earth', created by God 'in the beginning' are the totality of all things in the poet's mind. God who calls into being all that exists cannot be a being within that creation, however great a being God is meant to be. It is perhaps unhelpful to even talk about God 'existing', if God is to be thought of as the basis of existence.

What it seems to come to is a matter of whether we can visualize the universe which we experience as having any purposeful existence and development, or whether we see it simply as being here, without meaning or intrinsic value. To decide that, perhaps one has to ask oneself how it seems to be, how it feels, what kind of actions one view or the other can lead people into, and whether these fit with our sense of what matters.

Though this issue is not new, nor brought about by our current way of understanding the nature of the universe, our perception of its vastness and age can stretch our ability to believe that there is value in the actions of one life form on one small planet, let alone of individuals within the human race. But this expanded vision has not generated the difficulty.

Various writers in the Bible were aware of people who said that God did not know what they were doing and so they could get away with violence and injustice. These writers sometimes cried out in frustration because it seemed as if God did not notice. He certainly did not do anything obvious.

Their frustration was a declaration of their faith. It was because they believed that the poor and the weak mattered that they were angered by the injustices they suffered. If the oppressed had been of no importance there would have been no cry on their behalf. Similarly, there is a widespread unspoken sense in Western society that the world matters. It matters in itself, and the annihilation of species, the damage to its life systems and the spoiling of its beauty are wrong. The Hebrew view of the world corroborates this with a simple statement. The world does matter because it is God's creation. It matters to God.

The mindblowing size of the whole thing can be daunting and unsettling. Within a framework of infinity we can wonder how any part can have significance. We can wonder how specific parts can have any relative value. But in everyday life, when we are not beset by the great questions of meaning and purpose, we get on with living on the basis that specific things do matter. We generally reckon that size is not everything. At home we might have objects which take up very little space but which we value highly. In a garden there might be a plant which only flowers for a few days and then fades into the greenery, but we do not necessarily consider it a waste of space for that reason.

Again the talk of God is a corroboration of the assumption we make for life to continue, that things matter, and that some matter more than others. In talking about God as the Creator, one is saying that this is true of the cosmos as a whole, that what exists in one small corner for a short time still has value, and because God does not just exist but has purposes, then some things can have more value than others.

Hebrew thinking was that God could be specific, not only valuing the whole Creation, but choosing for his own purposes to develop a particular relationship with individuals or groups and giving them particular tasks. Humanity as a whole had a responsibility within the life of the earth; the Hebrews saw themselves as having a responsibility within humanity. An individual might also have a specific job to do, or be called by God to develop his or her potential in a certain way.

The fact that these kind of statements about God fit in with some of our basic assumptions and views does not necessarily mean that they are true. But they are not the kind of statement that can be proved. We are not dealing here with scientific or mathematical conclusions, nor with historical theories. Our understanding is that we live on this planet as part of a complex interconnection of life, moving around a small star, which in turn moves through infinite space.

The basic statement of the Bible is that this is all God's creation, that God values it, and that God has purposes within it. Here we are not dealing with understanding but with a kind of wisdom. It is a statement which may have a bearing on how we can live with each other and with the other life on this planet, and live well. Some writers in the Bible said that this perception was the very basis of wisdom. It is the kind of statement which is not open to proof, simply to assessment.

The Church's Failure

Thinking about the attitudes and actions of the Church down its history, it has to be admitted that it does not often seem to have shown a great respect for the rest of the created world. Its roots are there in the Hebrew writings of the Old Testament but as time went on it drew inspiration from other sources which were less positive about the world. The story is a complicated one, so any brief retelling will be a great simplification, but it needs to be told.

Jesus preached and taught about the 'kingdom of God'. Many Jews were looking forward to the coming of God's kingdom but they saw it in a number of different ways. Some expected a military rebellion against the Roman rulers and the establishment of a new Jewish state, ruled by God's Messiah. Others saw it as God's ending of history and bringing in a whole new world. Jesus' message seems to have been that the kingdom of God was breaking in as he actually preached, taught and healed. It was, he said, 'at hand', and people were, there and then, going into the kingdom.

So while Jesus also looked forward to some further action by God he would neither use violence to overthrow the Roman rule, nor write off the present world as a bad job to be destroyed or remade by God. Much of his teaching was in stories and images drawn from everyday life. He saw the ordinary things of his society and lifetime as pictures of God's activity.

> *Jesus said, 'What is the kingdom of God like?*
> *And to what should I compare it? It is like a mustard*
> *seed that someone took and sowed in the garden;*
> *it grew and became a tree,*
> *and the birds of the air made nests in its branches.'*
> *And again he said, 'To what should I compare*
> *the kingdom of God?*
> *It is like yeast that a woman took*
> *and mixed in with three measures of flour*
> *until all of it was leavened.'*
>
> Luke 13.18-21

As the Christian movement spread beyond Palestine it inevitably took different forms. People of different cultures came to see Jesus as significant for them, and the growing Church was quite clear: Jesus was for all people. People did not need to become Jews before they could be Christians. So the Christian movement took on board many different attitudes to life and some of these were quite pessimistic about the world.

Already amongst Jesus' contemporaries there was a hope of another or at least a new world, and this was taken into the Christian movement early on. Then, in the Greek speaking world, there were others who saw the world as basically a mess, or even a bad place, from which the human soul must be rescued. And while Christian teachers argued vehemently that it was Jesus who was the one who rescued people rather than some other saviour, they sometimes came to speak a similar language with a similar outlook on life.

In the fourth century, after many periods of violent persecution, Christianity came to be favoured by the emperor and much of the Roman establishment. It was a time of peace and consolidation for the Church. But fifty years later the state of the empire was getting precarious and people began to get very anxious about life. They feared the whole social order could collapse, and finally the Roman order did. But by that time a negative view of the world had taken a firm hold in much of the Church, and it stayed there in the following centuries. This left the way open for those with a desire to exploit the world regardless of what the consequences were for other life forms and future generations. The Church, revelling in its sense of value as the chosen people of God, neglected its responsibility to the rest of the life on earth, and to the Creator.

It seems to me that now, in order to be true to its roots, the Church needs to learn to appreciate and enjoy the beauty and mystery of the world, to recognize the Spirit of God within the life of the world, to see the human body as an aspect of the whole person which should be valued, and to struggle for all humanity to be granted the value and possibilities which are its due as the image of God. The Church also needs to help others see that this living planet is something entrusted to our care, to listen to and work with others who have seen that but perhaps do not use God-talk to express it, and to help in the hard decision-making and adjustments which are needed for the healing of the damaged earth to become something more than words and dreams. There are clear signs that this is happening in places.

An increasing number of Christians are involved in various aspects of the green movement. Various churches have produced studies and reports to help in Christian thinking about ecological issues. There is a considerable amount of theological work going on to interpret the whole concept of the universe as creation in terms which will correlate with our present scientific understanding. In many different quarters people are developing patterns and styles of prayer and worship which begin with an affirmation of the world as created and good, drawing from the prayers of churches in the past which were more positive about the world, or from other religions which hold to a view of the world as essentially valuable, or drawing on their own creativity.

The suggested reading and contacts in the appendices give some information which may be helpful to anyone wanting to take this further. Meanwhile we turn to think further about Jesus' teaching and action, and particularly his healing work, with a sense of the human person as informed by the insights of psychology.

CHAPTER FOUR
BETWEEN TWO WORLDS

OVERVIEW

THE EXPLORATION OF THE UNCONSCIOUS
THE WORLD OF JESUS OF NAZARETH
JESUS THE TEACHER
JESUS THE HEALER AND CURRENT PSYCHOLOGY
THE INFLUENCE OF MEMORIES
PARENT AND CHILD
THE NURTURING PARENT AND THE CREATIVE CHILD

The Exploration of the Unconscious

A friend of mine once had a poster with the slogan: 'The greatest area of unexplored territory is under your own hat'. The picture I recall was of a chimpanzee in a boater, but that was not really relevant to the possible truth of the statement. It is certainly the case that human exploration within the last century has not only been outwards, beyond the planet, but also inwards, into the human mind, and in that area there remain many unsolved mysteries. It is almost as if our consciousness is at the interface between two worlds. Beyond us and outside, stretching into the universe is the physical world which we know ourselves to be a part of. Within our minds are images, drives, dreams, and unknown forces which are also us, but another world.

Ways of understanding the workings of the mind have developed significantly during the last century, particularly following the work of Sigmund Freud in producing a coherent theory out of a number of other separate ideas which had developed in the nineteenth century. Freud laid the foundations of modern psychoanalysis and psychotherapy.

With the development of psychotherapy during the twentieth century there have been many splits and disagreements, and therapists today will use a number of quite different approaches. Those who follow C. G. Jung will be particularly interested in the dreams and fantasies of the client. Followers of Carl Rogers will focus on developing a rapport between patient and therapist, and see the attention the therapist pays the client as the crucial element in the healing work. Some will expect therapy to take place over a period of months or years, others will believe that useful work can be done in one session. Despite differences they will all tend to borrow techniques from different approaches and understandings of therapy, and hold some things in common.

Psychology has become a growth industry in the latter part of the twentieth century, not just in the number of people who visit psychotherapists for treatment but in the production of television documentaries and books on this field of knowledge. Beyond this are a multitude of workshops and programmes for personal growth, and a large number of stress counsellors are now employed in various areas of industry and commerce. Then there are films and novels which do not just tell what happens but explore the motives and the mind of the characters involved. Even a lot of gossip will be speculation as to why a certain person might have done something or what made them the person they are. And even while there are people who write psychology off as nonsense or pseudo-science, this interest in the minds and emotions of others and of ourselves is part of the cultural air we breathe in Western society.

A generally accepted psychological concept is that of the unconscious. In fact this is so widely accepted now that it must be considered a key image in much current Western thinking. It is accepted that the conscious mind, the part of our thinking and feeling of which we are aware, is only the tip of an iceberg. Underneath is a vast unconscious mind, a store of memories and fantasies, and a multitude of processes working away unrecognized by us, much as the heart and other organs continue to work within us without our noticing.

For Freud, the unconscious was the home of basic instinctual drives and correcting mechanisms, and problems occurred when the struggles between these generated too much pressure. For Jung the individual unconscious was linked at a great depth to a wider collective unconscious, and within the unconscious was a creative force, striving for the integration and growth of the individual person.

Much psychology will involve an exploration of the unconscious, though not all. Many people will speculate on the meaning of their dreams or the possible causes of odd behaviour in themselves or others, though without taking this far. It is widely accepted that there is more to us than meets the eye — that there are things that go on within our minds that we are not aware of, but which are probably significant. It is also widely accepted that people should, to some degree, be able to fulfil themselves — that some of the aspirations, hopes and possibilities of individual people should be realized.

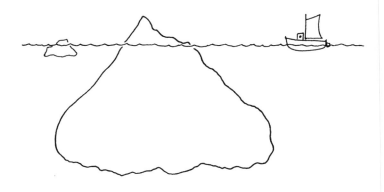

The World of Jesus of Nazareth

Another way that we might have a sense of being between two worlds is when we try to get our imaginations into the life and characters of another culture and period of history. Though the physical world was much the same, it was seen differently, and people were understood and related to in ways that might contrast with our own.

Jesus worked in Galilee during the early years of the Roman Empire. He was Jewish, accepting the books of the Law, the Prophets and the Writings as authoritative scriptures, and belonged to a society with values and expectations very different from those of twentieth century Europeans. In his society individual fulfilment was not valued. The individual person was a part of society, and was generally thought and felt to have significance because of the recognition granted by others. 'Honour' was a key word, not only in Jewish but in other Mediterranean societies of the time. It was also not a society which was greatly interested in the workings of the individual mind. What mattered a great deal to people was how they were thought of by others, and people understood themselves in terms of others' opinions. To some degree this is true of our society, but we also tend to understand ourselves and others in terms of what is going on in our minds and our emotions. People of the first-century Mediterranean culture told stories and wrote books but these stories were about what happened, out there. Our interest in what is going on in people's minds, in their motives and their feelings, was not a part of their interest. This creates a cultural gap between the people of Jesus' time and ourselves. In this chapter we will attempt to bridge that gap.

Jews saw themselves as part of the people of God, chosen by God for a special relationship with himself, and given the Law so that, in keeping it, they could live out a life which reflected God's values and ideals for the world. Their standing, not only in the eyes of other people, but also in the eyes of God, was important to them. And those in society who were in a position to say how God saw things were very influential and greatly respected.

The Jews of Galilee also lived in a precarious position. There was a great social difference between the rich and the poor. Though the people had folk memories of a time when each family had its own land, this was not the reality. Much of the land was now owned by absentee landlords, and the peasants struggled to survive as tenant farmers, craftsmen, fishermen, traders, or beggars.

The struggle was made harder by taxation. The Romans were there to keep the peace, but they demanded payment, and the system for collecting the taxes left plenty of scope for tax collectors to line their own pockets. The Romans were also pagans, believing in a number of gods, or effectively none at all. The only religious demand in the empire was that the emperor, the personalized spirit of Rome, be honoured as a god. Jews were exempt from this, but the thought was there all the time. God's people were under the rule of a person claiming deity for himself.

The Jews of Southern Palestine, Judea, were ruled directly by the Romans, and much Jewish religious practice was focused on the temple in Jerusalem. It was also in Jerusalem that one of the principal centres of Jewish study was located. Other centres were beyond

Palestine in cities of the Diaspora. Still, in Galilee, there were some trained Jewish scribes whose work was initially the copying of the scriptures, but also the interpretation and teaching of the Law. These people would be addressed as rabbi, or teacher, as might others who had not had the formal training but had acquired respect as a teacher.

There was also a strong movement, among the middle classes, of people calling themselves Pharisees. Their conviction was that they should set an example in the keeping of the Law, and that if others kept it in the same way then many of their people's problems would be solved. It was in this context that Jesus did his work. He was seen as a teacher, and a healer, and sometimes as the Messiah. Jesus seems not to have been keen to be spoken of in public as the Messiah, a matter which we will turn to later when we consider some features of what Jesus being the Messiah might mean.

Jesus also often told people to keep quiet about their healing experience, though he accepted the healing as an important side of what he was doing. It was not a separate task from his teaching and, in his own understanding, he seems to have seen both as aspects of the rule of God. His teaching, healing and messiahship were all part and parcel of the same thing. However we can consider them as different aspects of his work and deal with each of them in turn — teacher, healer, and later, Messiah.

Jesus the Teacher

We will turn in the next chapter to some aspects of what Jesus taught but at this point it will be valuable to focus for a moment on how he taught. We do not have verbatim accounts of his words, or eyewitness reports of his actions, recorded for posterity at the time of utterance or of action. We have four gospels, written by some of his earliest disciples, who collated what they had heard or seen, retold them many times, and then, thirty years or so later, wrote down these events.

The four gospels are not the same, and the Church in later centuries resisted moves to make one definitive gospel. There is a difference of detail, of emphasis and of interest on the part of the writers. We might say that what we have is Matthew's Jesus, Mark's Jesus, Luke's Jesus and John's Jesus. But these are not four different Jesuses. They are not inconsistent with each other in character or attitude, nor significantly different in terms of what he does. They are perhaps like looking through four different windows into the same room. We cannot get into the room, but we can have a clear idea of what it is like inside. In fact we can have a better idea than if we had just one window.

A great deal of work has been done to try to track back to what Jesus of Nazareth actually said — to the words of the man himself. This work has come up with some intriguing conclusions about what Jesus could well have said, though here we do not have the space to go into details. However this research has produced evidence that would stand the test of any historical enquiry and it shows that we are not dealing here with a figment of a collective imagination. Behind the gospels is the man, Jesus, a teacher and healer who was condemned and executed by the authorities for subversive activity.

Behind the gospels is Jesus of Nazareth. In the gospels we have the writings of some of his first followers, and it is those writings we will work with as we consider Jesus teaching. It would be possible to say every time, 'Jesus, according to Matthew, says ... etc', but that could become tedious so, for the sake of simplicity, I will refer simply to the words as Jesus' words.

In the gospels there are four significant features of the way Jesus taught:

(i) He taught authoritatively. What people were used to was a rabbi giving an opinion by quoting several others and then perhaps drawing his own learned conclusion. But Jesus did not say that according to rabbi x, this means p and q, whereas rabbi y has said something else. Jesus just said it. And sometimes he specifically laid it on the line. 'You have heard that it was said, "An eye for an eye and a tooth for a tooth", but I say to you...' Or, often in John's Gospel, 'Truly, truly, I say to you...' [1]

(ii) He also taught in parables. Some of these, like the Good Samaritan and the Prodigal Son, have entered the general pool of tales of Western society. Many people who have never read the books will be familiar with the phrases — 'Good Samaritan', or 'using one's talent', or 'hiding one's light under a bushel'. The familiarity of these stories is not always helpful because they can then come with a pre-packaged meaning, which may actually be different from what the gospel writer intended.

But apart from these well-known tales Jesus' teaching is littered with parable. Time and again things are put in terms of an activity or an event which on first hearing has nothing whatsoever to do with the subject in hand. But it does. Like a good joke the significance of the saying explodes with meaning half a second after it has been told. Or the parable works away in the imagination, shedding light on dark or cloudy ideas. And like a joke it is possible to miss the point completely.

Jesus was not alone in using parables. They were and still are a well-used teaching or provocative technique in many cultures. Jesus, however, seems to have developed the parable into a fine art.

(iii) Jesus also came out with short sayings: odd statements which seem perhaps to be paradoxical. For example, 'The kingdom of God is at hand.' 'Blessed are those who mourn, for they will be comforted.' 'Let the dead bury their own dead.' 'Give to the emperor the things that are the emperor's, and to God the things that are God's.' [2]

Like the parables, these are sayings that the hearer not only has to receive, but also has to deal with. Like cryptic crossword clues they sit in the mind and need puzzling over. Sometimes they throw out light, sometimes they disturb and sometimes they might be dismissed as nonsense. Like the parables, these kind of sayings establish a curious relationship between the teacher and the hearer. This is significant; Jesus taught authoritatively, but generally he was not berating people nor battering them into agreement with what he said. He was telling stories or making statements which the hearer then had to accept, and to work with, or to discard. The hearer's own integrity was not threatened.

(iv) Jesus also made statements which are described as apocalyptic. Apocalyptic writing was a popular genre of the time, and although most people did not read the books, they were into the apocalyptic way of thinking and talking about things. Apocalyptic literature was basically coded, and fantastic, and the main theme was that this was a time of significant struggle between the forces of darkness and the power of God, and God was about to act decisively. There were whole religious movements which were preparing themselves for the great fray.

Jesus on occasion spoke in these terms particularly when he was asked by his disciples about the future of Jerusalem. It is impossible to say how much of this comes from Jesus of Nazareth, and how much of it is an elaboration of what Jesus actually said: the sayings of Jesus gathering further material like a snowball rolling down a hill. There is less of it in Mark's gospel, the earliest, than in Matthew or Luke, and none in John.

Jesus the Healer and Current Psychology

As we have said, Jesus' society was not given to introspection or to valuing individual expression, and the accounts that we have of Jesus in the gospels are the product of such a society. The fourth gospel, John, has long reflective passages about the significance of Jesus' life and work. The other three tell what Jesus said and did. They were not interested in what was going on in the mind of Jesus, nor of those he met. Even if they had had that interest, they would have used different concepts from those which are common currency in the late twentieth century.

The gospel writers tell us about how Jesus dealt with people, so if we are to try to interpret Jesus' work with people into the terms of our own society, then we will need to use an approach which honours this interest and concern of the gospel writers. In other words we will have to use an approach which deals with what happens, rather than what people feel or imagine.

It would be possible to speculate on the thoughts and feelings of the participants, and even on their unconscious drives and disturbances. A historical novelist might do this to good effect. But it would be moving beyond what the gospel texts actually give us, and we would do better to consider them using a psychological approach which works from what happens and can be observed.

One such approach is that known as 'Transactional Analysis'. It was developed by Eric Berne in the United States in the 1950s, and has come to be widely used by psychotherapists of many different schools, and also by management and group work trainers. The principles are relatively simple and, as the name suggests, it works by considering firstly how people relate to each other, rather than how they are feeling or thinking, or what they dream or imagine. We will look now at the basic ideas of this approach, and then in the next chapter move on to consider some descriptions of Jesus' activity in the light of this.

The Influence of Memories

Some people are able to recall what happened to them at a very early age. Others have difficulty remembering much at all from their childhood. But what sometimes happens is that a person suddenly remembers something they had once forgotten. A sound, a sight, a smell, or perhaps nothing obvious at all brings into mind a scene or a situation from long ago which the person could not have deliberately recalled.

What is generally accepted now is that our minds store up everything that happens to us, but only some of it is accessible. It is like information stored on a computer, much of it in files which cannot now be accessed. Of course things happen which might damage the hardware — aging, injury or disease — and whatever was there is either erased or cannot be retrieved. But mostly the material is there, in the unconscious mind, and the conscious mind cannot, or chooses not to recall it. The memories, however, though not accessible to the conscious mind, still affect the person.

We can take three common examples of this:

Many people experience difficulty relating to their parents even when they are adults. Someone may be in their forties and have lived independently for twenty years, dealing with all sorts of people of different ages. When a request or a demand is made by a parent they behave quite differently. They may find themselves complying with quite unreasonable requests, or unable to contradict statements which they know to be wrong.

Some people have difficulty in not working. Whenever they stop they feel guilty. Others who suffer with this kind of guilt drive get into a double bind. They also feel guilty when they do not stop working, because they feel they ought to spend time with their families.

Other people have difficulty in relationships because they cling on to another person, afraid that their friend or partner is going to leave them, and so actually make the relationship harder by their possessiveness. And, of course, there are many people who have none of these problems and others who have trouble with all three.

What is happening in all of these common situations is that memories of long ago are playing in the background, like supermarket music which is not heard but affects the mood of the shopper. With the person who has difficulty relating to their parent, what is happening is that the voice of the parent in the present time is resonating with the memories of the parent voice long ago, when the parent was big and powerful and the child was weak and dependent.

Often, when the workaholic stops, it is as if there are voices telling him that he is a waster who needs to prove himself by achieving great things. The voice is there, perhaps below the level of consciousness: but a memory, or accumulation of memories, of long ago. The memories may be of things actually said by parents or teachers, or they may be expressions of face or body which created a sense of worthlessness within the child the person was and which they are still struggling to deny. But there may be no-one to give the reward. The parent or the forceful teacher has gone away, beyond reach, but their criticism is still there in the memory.

The person in the double bind of guilt has memories giving conflicting messages. They might have memories which drive them to keep busy and try to achieve great things, but also messages telling them they need to stop, relax, be with their family, be a good caring parent to their own children. And they cannot do both.

The possessive adult is haunted by childhood experience, often unrecognized but powerful; the memories of the parent who left, or threatened to; or the parent who sulked, cutting themself off until they got their own way or were pandered to with other concessions.

Parent and Child

The experiences of our early months and years are stored in our memories as two kinds of information. There are experiences from the outside: the voices, looks, touch and expressions, of significant figures, particularly parents. There are also the memories of what those situations were like from the inside: the feelings of being shouted at, laughed at, cuddled or left. In Transactional Analysis these sets of memories are referred to as the Parent memories, and the Child memories. And the person is guided or pulled by these two sets of memories.

What also hopefully happens is that a person develops their own identity and the ability to decide things for themself. They may hear the Parent voice in their mind but choose to do differently. They may decide to do a particular thing even though there is a feeling of anxiety or fear arising from the influence of the Child memories within them. This independent faculty which hears the voices but makes its own decisions is referred to as the Adult. Diagrammatically these are often drawn as three circles: P, A and C, and as a shorthand the three initial letters are often used. Capital letters are always used in this imagery as the Parent is not the literal parent of the person, but memories, many of which probably, but not necessarily, come from the parents.

The idea behind Transactional Analysis is that these modes of operation are clearly seen in transactions between people and, if transactions are observed and analysed, a person can see what they and others are doing.

Sometimes a short dialogue takes place in which two people relate from the Adult mode:

'What's the time?'

'Two thirty.'

A short, simple, straight answer.

It could be a longer dialogue:

'Did you do anything interesting last night?'

'Yes, I saw a fascinating television programme about the way they train prospective professional footballers. What they do is...'

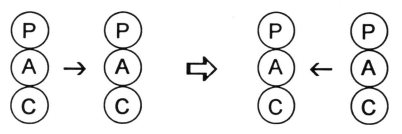

But sometimes it is not like that:

'What's the time?'

'Time you got a watch!'

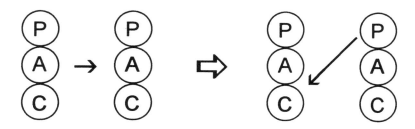

This time the first person is coming from their A but the reply comes from the P. It is an attempt to put the other one down, who may reply from their A:

'I have one actually. I just want to check it is correct. Do you have a problem?'

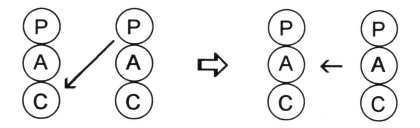

Or they might buckle under and reply from their C:

'Sorry. I only wanted to see if it was right.'

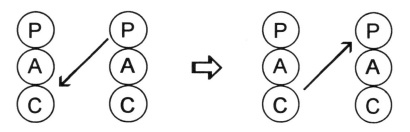

Or they might move into their P mode and try to score one off the other person:

'Time you learnt to be civil. Just because you got out of bed the wrong side doesn't mean you can ...'

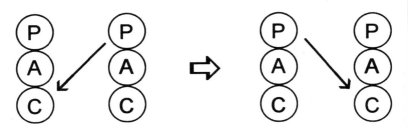

These modes of operation, the P, A and C, are known as ego-states. They are there in each person, and each person operates out of different ego-states at different times, although some people have a tendency to one mode more than to others. Politicians who speak to the populace as if they are small children are operating largely from the P mode. The person who is continually apologizing for speaking, interrupting, or simply existing, is largely operating in the C ego-state. A person who generally addresses other people on the level, neither trying to put them down nor treating the others as if they are somehow more significant, is probably operating largely from their A.

The Nurturing Parent and the Creative Child

The memories which form the ego-states are not all bad. Parent figures do not only shout and threaten or leave when the child wants

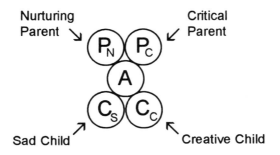

them around. They also do all sorts of things to comfort and encourage children. Similarly, a person's childhood experience is hopefully not all bad. There were perhaps also times of exploration, play and creativity. The existence of the good and the bad memories means that the human mind can be thought of as having five, rather than three ego-states. There is a Nurturing and a Critical Parent, a Sad and a Creative Child, and an Adult.

What happens when people relate to each other is a double process. A person moves into an ego-state, rather like putting on a costume. For a short while they become a Nurturing or Critical Parent, or a Sad or Creative Child, or their own Adult self. What they also do is project onto others one of these states, so that a person in the Sad Child mode may well project onto another person who seems interested in them, the dress of the Nurturing Parent, and relate to them in that way. The other person may accept that, and play the game. If they reject it, they might cause distress to the Sad Child, but they may help the person move out of that mode into their Adult, depending on how the refusal is handled.

Sometimes it is appropriate for a person to operate from one of their Parent ego-states, or their Child ego-states. One has responsibilities to care for others, and a potential for being creative and original. In carrying out these responsibilities and using this potential, a person is often operating from their Parent or Child ego-states.

The aim of Transactional Analysis is to help people be aware of how they engage with others and to operate from the state that is appropriate for the situation, thus putting the Adult in charge. In so doing, the people involved will be freed from the domination of past experiences. The memories are not wiped out, it is simply that with understanding and practice they can deal with them and live their own lives in the present time, rather than rehearse old scripts of plays long past.

There is disagreement as to how much the ego-states are simply the results of accumulated memories, and how much they are more basic: whether they are programmes built up from one's own experience or whether there is some pre-programming of the person. Young children and animals respond to stroking and other physical encouragements. If deprived of this they mentally withdraw, and will ultimately die. This fundamental need seems to be built into the animal. The ability to explore and play also seems to be there from the beginning. Children do not need to be taught how to play, though they will finally stop if continually discouraged by parent figures.

It may be that the mental structure is there in humans for them to form these ego-states, though at the beginning of life they have little or no content. With that may go the necessary mental structure to develop an ethical sense. A person's sense of right and wrong will vary considerably from culture to culture, but the possibility of developing one could well be part of the mental equipment we are born with. What is generally accepted in most schools of psychotherapy is that early experiences influence a person profoundly. The Transactional Analysis approach provides a clear way of seeing how that influence works out in practice.

The Transactional Analysis theory is much more developed than this brief outline might suggest, leading into ways of understanding severe personality disorders and relationship difficulties. But we will turn now to consider some of Jesus' dealings with people, using the Transactional Analysis approach as a key image for understanding what Jesus is doing.

1   Quotes are from Matthew 5:38; John 3:5.
2   Quotes are from Mark 1:15; Matthew 5:4; Matthew 8:22; Matthew 22 :21.

Chapter Five
The Cycle of Healing

Overview

Jesus in Action

The gospels are full of Jesus' encounters with people, but many of these are told very briefly. In order to analyse how, according to the gospel writers, Jesus related to people we will consider four stories which are told in some detail. There is still sometimes not the detail we would wish for but there is enough to develop a general picture. We are inevitably making a small selection of the possible episodes, but the general picture these give can be checked out by reading others.

• *A man with a crippled hand*

Early on in Mark's Gospel Jesus gets into conflict over what is permissible on the Sabbath day:

> *Jesus entered the synagogue, and a man was there*
> *who had a withered hand. The Pharisees watched*

*him to see whether he would cure him on the sabbath,
so that they might accuse him. And he said to the
man who had the withered hand, 'Come forward.'
Then he said to them, 'Is it lawful to do good or to
do harm on the sabbath, to save life or to kill?' But
they were silent.*

*He looked around at them with anger; he was
grieved at their hardness of heart and said to the
man, 'Stretch out your hand.'*

He stretched it out, and his hand was restored.

*The Pharisees went out, and immediately conspired
with the Herodians against him, how to destroy him.*

(Mark 3:1–6)

Often the ego-state of a person can be told from their body language: the stance of the Critical Parent is different from that of the
Nurturing Parent; the Creative Child is bright eyed and fast moving;
the Sad Child is slow, perhaps with head bowed or face hidden.

Here we cannot see the body language, but we are told what is going on. The Pharisees are in Critical Parent mode, and their criticism
is towards both Jesus, who might heal on the Sabbath, and towards
the man, who might be hoping for something which is against the
Law as they interpret it.

Jesus calls the man forward. The man now has to decide whether or
not to come. There are conflicting voices in this room, and no doubt
in his mind. The Pharisees have tradition behind them. The man has
probably been brought up with their way of seeing things, and respect for them and their ways would have been developed in him from
an early age. But then there is Jesus who has another reputation. And
there is also his own desire to get well.

Jesus then throws out an ironic question. He does not engage in
argument with the Pharisees; he straightforwardly challenges them to
think again. In a way this cuts the Pharisees off from the sick man. It
is as if Jesus has pushed the Pharisees back from him and given him
space. Then, having cut them off, he tells the man to do what he could
not do before: to stretch out his hand. The man now does it, and is
well; the Pharisees are not pleased. We do not know what was going
on in the man's mind, or Jesus', though we are told something of how
he felt. And we can see the process that led to the man's healing.

• *A woman with a haemorrhage*

Some time later in the same gospel, Jesus is approached for help by a ruler of the synagogue, a significant leader of the local community. He asks Jesus to heal his daughter and Jesus sets off towards his house. On the way he is approached by a woman who also needs help:

> *There was a woman who had been suffering with haemorrhages for twelve years. She had endured much under many physicians, and had spent all that she had; and she was no better, but rather grew worse. She had heard about Jesus, and came up behind him in the crowd and touched his cloak. For she said, 'If I but touch his garments, I will be made well.'*
>
> *Immediately the haemorrhage stopped; and she felt in her body that she was healed of her disease.*
>
> *Immediately aware that power had gone forth from him, Jesus turned about in the crowd, and said, 'Who touched my clothes?'*
>
> *And his disciples said to him, 'You see the crowd pressing in on you; how can you say, "Who touched me?"'*
>
> *He looked all around to see who had done it.*
>
> *But the woman, knowing what had been done to her, came in fear and trembling, fell down before him, and told him the whole truth.*
>
> *He said to her, 'Daughter, your faith has made you well; go in peace, and be healed of your disease.'*
>
> (Mark 5:25–34)

According to Jewish Law and custom of the time a menstruating woman should keep to herself. If the menstruation continued beyond the normal period she would be considered unclean until a week after the bleeding had finished, then she could be certified clean and re-enter society. This seems to have been the woman's problem. Not only would she have been weak from anaemia but also unable to mix with people in the normal way as she would have contaminated them with her uncleanness. So she should not have been out in the crowd. She should not have deliberately touched Jesus. And to make it worse, the man who was with Jesus was the ruler of the synagogue, whose job it was to make sure that these kind of laws and customs were kept.

However Jesus was reputed to be a healer who had time for social rejects, and regardless of law and custom she went out, pushed through the crowd, and touched him to be healed. Naturally she wanted to keep it quiet. She had contaminated many people in the crowd, and Jesus, who was on his way to help the ruler of the synagogue. But Jesus will not have this secrecy. Whoever has touched him must acknowledge it, and he waits for the culprit to own up. She does so, terrified.

Jesus will not have the woman stay in her C ego-state. She must boldly acknowledge what she, of her own will and against custom and law, decided to do. He relates to her A, and she responds in that way, despite her fears.

Jesus then explains that her faith was instrumental in the healing. Whatever 'power' he had, it required her faith to allow the healing to happen. Faith here, as throughout the New Testament, is not a set of beliefs but a trust. Jesus does not quiz her about what she believes about God, or himself. He recognizes that she trusts he will not harm her but heal her. That is her faith.

The story goes on that a messenger arrives to tell the ruler of the synagogue that his daughter has died. With the shock of this news, and the fact that Jesus the healer has not only been delayed by the woman, but also contaminated by her, Jesus tells the ruler to trust him. He, the ruler of the synagogue, is to do what the ill and unclean woman did.

The woman, as well as being healed, becomes an example for a person whom everything else in her culture and in her mind told her was superior to her.

• A woman accused of unlawful sex

There is an occasion when a woman is actually used by the Pharisees and scribes in an attempt to catch Jesus out:

> *Early in the morning Jesus came again to the temple.*
> *All the people came to him, and he sat down and*
> *began to teach them.*
>
> *The scribes and Pharisees brought a woman who*

*had been caught in adultery; and making her stand
before all of them, they said to him, 'Teacher, this
woman has been caught in the very act of commit-
ting adultery. Now in the law Moses commanded us
to stone such people. Now what do you say?'*

*This they said to test him, so that they might have
some charge to bring against him.*

*Jesus bent down and wrote with his finger on the
ground.*

*When they kept on questioning him, he straightened
up and said to them, 'Let anyone among you who is
without sin be the first to throw a stone at her.'*

*And once more he bent down and wrote on the
ground.*

*When they heard it, they went away, one by one,
beginning with the elders; and Jesus was left alone
with the woman standing before him.*

*Jesus straightened up and said to her, 'Woman,
where are they? Has no-one condemned you?'*

She said, 'No-one, sir.'

*And Jesus said, 'Neither do I condemn you; go your
way, and from now on do not sin again.'*

(John 8:2–11)

We do not know why Jesus wrote on the ground. Perhaps he was
writing names of people he knew things about. Perhaps he was just
occupying his hands to help him contain his anger. Of course it takes
two to commit adultery, but this was a man's world and it is the woman
they have dragged along to try to catch him out. Adultery in Jewish
Law was not an offence against a person but an offence of property.
Having sex with another man's wife meant you were misusing his
property and possibly contaminating his line of descent with your
seed. Whoever had been having sex with this woman was not com-
mitting adultery against his wife, if he had one, but against the woman's husband, if she had one.

They reckoned it was a case for stoning. The Jews were not allowed by the Romans to carry out stoning, but this was a test case, and if Jesus said to stone her, they could hand him over to the Roman police. If Jesus had said not to stone her they could have accused Jesus of teaching what was against the Law. Jesus might then have lost some of his following. But it did not work out either way. Jesus turned the whole thing round on them, and protected the woman.

There was also only one circumstance when stoning could be called for in a case of adultery. That was when the woman did not have a husband but was betrothed. In that case she was the pledged property of her husband to be, but this woman had now spoiled herself by having sex with someone else. She was now a waste, and a bad example who must be dealt with appropriately. We do not know who the man involved was, but there is the possibility that he was someone that she would have married if the choice had been hers and not her father's. That is speculation, but it is hard to think of likely alternatives.

Jesus' response to the situation is thoughtful, and deceptively simple. He does not allow himself to be cornered by these scribes and Pharisees, but neither does he flare up at them for their callousness and hypocrisy. He does not go into the Critical Parent mode, and out-Parent them, but operates from his Adult. This time with a cool challenge. They are free to stone her if they choose to. The choice is theirs. They only have to declare themselves sinless. They can rake back in their memories if they want to, but presumably most of them knew what they were up to, and knew enough about the compassion of God from their own study of the Prophets to realize that they were not in a position to continue.

Jesus does not berate the woman either. He refuses to condemn her, only to instruct her. Perhaps he is relating to her also in the Adult ego-state, perhaps as a Nurturing Parent. That we cannot tell without the tone of voice and the body language.

The Cycle of Healing

This process that Jesus engages in could be described as a Cycle of healing. In each case a person is being pushed into, or kept in, the Sad Child mode by the Critical Parent. The Law was a part of the upbringing of all these people who came before Jesus. The Pharisees and the ruler of the synagogue represent this Law, and in these situations are obstructing the person's healing or even wanting the person's destruction. They are operating in the Critical Parent mode and keeping, or pushing, the person down.

Jesus blocks off the Critical Parent, not by outdoing its criticism but by a question or challenge, or by demanding that the person move out of the Sad Child mode. He calls the man with the withered hand forward. He does not just treat him as a patient but demands that he take some action. We are not told whether or not the man moved against the wishes of the Pharisees, but he is then told by Jesus to stretch out his hand. It is something he has to do. Likewise the woman with the haemorrhage has to own up to her actions which are contrary to law and custom, and take responsibility for what she has done. She cannot slip quietly away like a child with a comfort. And Jesus addresses the woman, whom the Pharisees want to stone, with a question. He does not treat her with contempt, nor does he excuse what she has done. He simply tells her not to do it again.

In each case, Jesus blocks off the Critical Parent, taking on the role of a protector of the accused person. The person is then enabled to draw from the Nurturing Parent and go free. They become an Adult able to draw on the energy of the Creative Child.

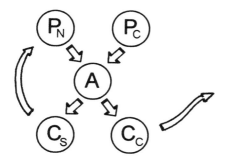

• *A paralysed man*

We see this again in another gospel passage:

> *When Jesus returned to Capernaum after some days,
> it was reported that he was at home. So many people
> gathered around that there was no longer room for
> them, not even in front of the door; and he was*

speaking the word to them. The some people came, bringing to him a paralysed man, carried by four of them. And when they could not bring him to Jesus because of the crowd, they removed the roof above him; and after having dug through it, they let down the mat on which the paralytic lay. When Jesus saw their faith, he said to the paralytic, 'Son, your sins are forgiven.'

Now some of the scribes were sitting there, questioning in their hearts, 'Why does this fellow speak in this way? It is blasphemy! Who can forgive sins but God alone?'

At once Jesus perceived in his spirit that they were discussing these questions among themselves; and he said to them, 'Why do you raise such questions in your hearts? Which is easier, to say to the paralytic, "Your sins are forgiven," or to say, "Stand up and take your mat and walk"? But so that you may know that the Son of Man has authority on earth to forgive sins' — he said to the paralytic — 'I say to you stand up, take your mat and go to your home.'

And he stood up, and immediately took the mat and went out before all of them; so that they were all amazed and glorified God, saying, 'We have never seen anything like this!'

(Mark 2:1–2)

This man cannot move at all. His friends have the courage to get him to Jesus regardless of the obstacles, even though it means damaging someone's property. Jesus recognizes their faith. They trust that Jesus has as much concern for their friend as they do, perhaps more.

Despite all its frustrations and humiliations, being unable to move does mean that you do not have to make decisions, and you cannot do things wrong. When the man is in front of him Jesus tells him his sins are forgiven. These wrong things that he has done are in the past. Now is a new moment and a new opportunity. But the man does not move. The scribes are there, and they are muttering; they are critical of Jesus but Jesus does not accept the criticism. He responds with a comic challenge: 'Which is easier to say?' The complaint was not about what is easy, but what is right. Jesus will not be deterred by this and it is clear to the man on the mat that Jesus is not being put down by the Pharisees.

The man on the mat then hears a challenge for himself. 'I say to you, stand up, take your mat, and go to your home.' Being told his sins are forgiven is one thing. That is comforting. It comes from a Nurturing Parent. But now he must respond in the Adult mode. Jesus tells him to get up. If he does so he is ignoring the criticism of the scribes, and the whole weight of stultifying past criticism which their muttering conjures up. He has to make a decision. He gets up, picks up his mat and goes out.

We cannot see what is going on in the man's mind and body in this healing story, but we can see what is going on between the people involved. The Critical Parent scribes are blocked off and the Sad Child man is able to respond to the Nurturing Parent Jesus. But then he must decide as an Adult, what he does.

The Context of Healing

This does not explain how the healing of these people came about. In most, if not all situations, the processes of healing remain something of a mystery. In the case of a cut finger, it is not clear why the cells of the skin, muscle and blood vessels develop and reproduce to form something that resembles what was there before the injury was done. Whether or not someone will pull through after a major operation is sometimes very hard to predict. In hospitals, as well as homes and other places of healing, there are many instances of recovery which were unexpected by those caring for the ill or injured person. Often how the healing came about remains unknown. All that is known are some of the circumstances surrounding the recovery, which may be relevant.

This is the kind of thing we have here. These stories describe Jesus' dealings with people. From the angle we have looked at them we can recognize a pattern in the way Jesus relates to the participants, which we have described as a healing cycle. My suggestion is that this is relevant to the healing process whether we are concerned with the healing of bodies, minds or relationships.

In fact this kind of separation of bodies, minds and relationships is sometimes unhelpful even in understanding what appears to be a simple problem. Many general practitioners are aware that the problem that a patient presents to them as a physical ailment has causes or contributing factors which lie in their minds or their relationships. Home life, work stress, personality disorders rooted in past experience; all these interplay with each other. A doctor might see principally a physical ailment; that is often what presents itself, and it is what people mainly expect doctors to deal with. But often the doctor is aware that other dimensions of the person's life have a significant part to play. Sometimes this might be simple: overeating leading to physical disorders, but which stems from finding comfort in filling the mouth with food; a tendency to be accident-prone arising from an inability to concentrate, which results from a number of anxieties; illnesses or disabilities possibly created unconsciously because they generate sympathy and gain attention from other people which might not come otherwise. However, often connections are much more complex and, though suspected, are difficult or impossible to track down with the limited time and resources available to a general practitioner.

This way of seeing various dimensions of a person's life as relevant to their health or healing is not new, but it is something which has become more pronounced within our society in the last few decades. Some alternative therapists have emphasized this and are sometimes described as practising forms of holistic medicine; but it is not only outside mainstream Western medicine that this sense of interconnectedness has developed. It is likely to go further and, as some of the proponents of alternative medicine are quick to point out, this holistic sense is something which was characteristic of many approaches to healing before and beyond the development of Western scientific medicine. It was certainly true of the Mediterranean world of Jesus' time and of earlier Hebrew thinking. We saw in chapter three how, in one of the creation stories of Genesis, the first man is created as a living being and it was fundamental to the Old Testament writers that the person was a multidimensional whole, and not, as in some world views, a soul inhabiting a body.

So it is that when Jesus speaks to a paralysed man and tells him that his sins are forgiven, it might seem to us that he is missing the obvious point. The man was brought because he could not move. Jesus talks about his past behaviour; but to the people with whom Jesus was dealing, this would not have seemed obscure. Past actions, a present sense of guilt and failure, and potential for further action, would all have been linked in people's minds together with thoughts about the paralysed man's present relationships, his standing in the community, and his feelings. They would have thought of him as a whole being within a network of relationships. What we have focused on is the way Jesus intervened in that network to release the man's potential.

The pattern which we saw in Jesus' dealings with people on several occasions can be, and is, repeated in many other situations. The catalyst for this kind of process could be almost anyone. A therapist or counsellor is an obvious candidate, but a friend or partner could also fulfil the role taken by Jesus in these transactions.

The ultimate aim of a therapist using Transactional Analysis will be for the person to be able to work through the process on their own. The therapist will not be wanting the person to develop a long term dependence on the therapist or a support group. In a similar way it is noticeable how Jesus time and again told people he had healed to go away: 'Take your mat and go home,' 'Go in peace, and be healed.'

A person might go through the cycle without outside help, and this is what a therapist using Transactional Analysis will be working for in the long term. In the terminology of one proponent of this approach, the therapist will be helping the person be able to move from a Sad Child state to knowing 'I'm OK', and to recognizing the other as being 'OK' as well. But often people do need help to do this, whether it is by someone with training or a friend who simply helps them see things differently.

Stages and Obstacles in the Healing Cycle

There will be three key stages in this healing process:

1. The Welcome

The person in the Sad Child ego-state needs to be welcomed by another, or to be able to accept themselves in the state they are in. Among many counsellors and therapists this is seen as the key aspect of their work. Carl Rogers believed that the 'unconditional positive regard' of the counsellor for the client was the key factor in any healing work.

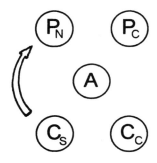

The people in these gospel episodes have all been welcomed by Jesus. He has not rejected them. Their faith has been their trusting that this would happen.

2. The Workout

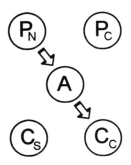

There needs to be a process of working out what is happening: why they are as they are; what has triggered off this state; or even simply recognizing the state they are in and being able to think about it objectively rather than be immersed in it. A counsellor using Transactional Analysis will help their client move from thinking about the transactions in a situation to their feelings that gave rise to their response, and to how these possibly inappropriate feelings may have arisen. There are a multitude of other approaches to counselling, psychotherapy and physical healing, but they all involve some way of either working out the root of the problem, or of working with the problem to resolve it.

In the gospels Jesus also has dealings with these people. The woman who wants to creep away quietly is not allowed to. The man with the withered hand is challenged by Jesus to respond. The man on the mat is told he is forgiven, and then challenged to move against the criticism of the Pharisees. There is some kind of work going on here; Jesus is not just making things better for the person without their involvement in the process.

3. The Departure

The person needs to be able then to leave the analysis, the reflection, or other healing work and go out — to run the risk of making more mistakes, of being hurt again, or of returning to the same state. But they have to go.

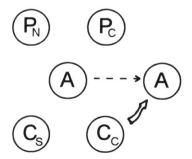

As we have already noted, Jesus does not keep these people with him. In some cases he specifically tells them to go; they are to get on with life.

We have suggested that Jesus' healing work involved a welcome, a workout and a departure, as would the work of other healers, be they therapists, counsellors, physicians or friends. It is possible, of course, that this three-stage cycle does not always occur, in which case the problem is not properly resolved. The person may remain in their unhealthy state or simply be moved into another one.

There can be blockages at any point in the process:

There might be no welcome. The therapist, the priest, the partner or the parent might demand that the person be better before they are acceptable, and the Sad Child is stuck.

There might be no workout. The response could be a bland 'Never mind' which does not get to the root of the problem and bring any enlightenment, or the person could be kept in their crippled state by a Parent figure who needs a Sad Child to continually bully or possessively care for.

There could then be no departure. The person might be kept in the Sad Child state, never able to leave the Parent figure and run the risks that go with being an Adult.

These can be seen clearly in the kind of situation where a person needs help from another with what presents itself as an emotional or psychological problem or a difficulty in relationships. These are the type of problems for which techniques like Transactional Analysis can often be of help. But it might also apply when the presenting problem is of a different kind. There are people who change their doctor because they are dissatisfied with the doctor's attitude towards them, and have a sense that they will do better with a doctor who treats them with more respect. And sometimes they are right. There are other people who follow alternative therapies with some success, and also suspect that this is the result of the attention that they are paid by the therapist, and that with the new therapist there is a more serious working at the problem. There are also times when a therapist and client work for a long time together but seem to make no progress until someone else points out to the therapist that they have come to need the client. Only when they are prepared to let the client go can the client really progress.

However, healing is a process of life which is not confined to the consulting room and the surgery. Therefore these blockages can occur in many situations which might have a potential for healing, but actually become a source of constraint and disability. There are friends and partners who do not accept each other as they are, so that each one is continually struggling to be acceptable to the other in appearance or behaviour. The outcome is a lack of spontaneity and peace. There are families where disagreements are never faced or awkward subjects are never broached, and relationships remain superficial or stilted. There are parents who dread the day when their child will actually leave the family home and who struggle, often unconsciously, to keep their children with them, dependent and tied.

Part of the way of things is that we all carry wounds with us from our past experience and these can lead to our relationships with other people being less than we would hope for. New things happen which cause distress and pain to us and to other people with whom we share our lives. Being healthy or whole is not something we can solve once and for all. But we can continually work at our own growth towards greater wholeness in ourselves and in our relationships with other people and with the world. We can also expect or hope to make or find groups where this process is encouraged.

The Church and the Healing Cycle

Down the centuries churches have been involved in healing work in a number of different ways. There was a period of centuries when the churches, either in monasteries or in their ordinary local life, were the principal agents for dealing with disease and injury. With the development of medicine in the last five centuries churches have moved onto the sidelines as organizations, although many of the leading practitioners and researchers were members of churches. In Western society, churches have also often provided chaplains to work alongside physicians, surgeons and nurses, and in their gatherings churches have usually prayed for people who were known to be unwell.

In recent decades there has been a renewed interest in healing as a part of what the church is about, with churches holding healing services and reviving ancient practices like the laying on of hands and anointing with oil. Elsewhere there has been an emphasis on healing at meetings with acknowledged 'healers', sometimes with extraordinary results claimed and publicized. This renewed interest can sometimes be a sign of churches changing their attitude to and understanding of life so that people are coming to be seen as a whole rather than an embodied soul, and physical life is now being seen as important in itself rather than as simply a preparation for a spiritual hereafter. In this, the attitude of churches can be seen as a part of a significant trend in Western society, or at least echoing what is happening elsewhere. Some churches would probably see their increased interest in the whole person, rather than the soul or spirit, as a development rooted in the Bible but also in sympathy with other trends towards a more holistic view of life.

However it does also have to be acknowledged that sometimes the interest in healing is more a kind of desire for religious fireworks, to make church meetings more exciting, or even the result of a kind of competitiveness which denigrates the work of scientific medicine in deference to the results of prayer, as if they were alternative possibilities. Sometimes churches with an emphasis on healing might even see themselves as providing an alternative to both mainstream medicine and other alternative therapies, which they might brand as dangerous or evil. But the concept of God as Creator which we explored in chapter three would point towards an acknowledgement of God being involved in all healing processes.

God the Creator does not work in competition with the creative and healing processes of the world but these very processes are brought into existence by God. There is not some other power which people can tap into which will remedy ailments and restore injuries. There is only the one God. As we saw earlier, the Spirit of God is not some kind of magic force that can be conjured up by earnest prayer, ardent belief or proper rituals, but is the life of the Creator working within the cosmos to generate and regenerate form, life and new potential.

Prayer and the Healing Cycle

We will think about prayer and worship in more depth in chapter seven but it is worth noting the way that the healing cycle can operate in prayer. There are a number of different forms of prayer, but, whatever form is being used, the three stages of the healing cycle might take place.

A person might feel that their praying is an attempt to communicate with God, perhaps to break through to the consciousness of an unheeding power. This kind of urgent pleading can be identified in places in the Psalms, the collection of written songs and prayers in the Old Testament. But the basis of praying is that the person is accepted by God. It may sometimes take a period of mental struggle for the person praying to realize this, but the logic is that the very possibility of prayer depends on the one to whom a person prays being open to them. Beginning to pray is an action of faith, like that of the woman with the haemorrhage who approached Jesus. One is only going to pray if one has at least some vague idea that it is worthwhile. The people who approached Jesus for help reckoned that it was worth a try. Jesus' disciples came to see his acceptance of these people as demonstrating the acceptance of God, which he also talked about.

A lot of praying does not take the form of presenting problems to God. Again, as with Jesus, not everyone who came to see him or talk with him was ill or aware of a need for healing. But once a person has begun to pray there might be a working out of a problem, a thinking over, or a talking over of something that has happened to them which puts them into the mode of the Sad Child. In some forms of prayer this might not be addressed directly. In meditation the person might simply remain still with their mind focused or open, or their thoughts moving around a phrase or a story. But here something can be going on unconsciously to restore a degree of harmony to the mind and emotions. There is a process taking place of refocusing, rearranging of ideas, priorities and feelings. It is a working out, but with a less focused or conscious part of the mind.

Then the person leaves their praying. They go out, to risk making more mistakes, sinning again, and getting hurt again. But there is a possibility of their going out to live freely, knowing that their acceptance by God is not dependent on their achievements, or their sinlessness, but that they are welcomed by God as they are.

Of course, prayer is not literally coming to God, but it is a focusing of the attention on God. So, when the attention switches, as it must, then a person is in a sense going out from God. The mind and attention are moving elsewhere. The ancient Hebrews, like many other peoples, had particular places where God was thought to be present — at shrines and especially, later, at the temple in Jerusalem. Their prayers in the Psalms speak of 'entering the presence of God', and they had a clear literal sense of going out from the holy place to the mundane. Nevertheless they also had a strong sense of God encountering people in other situations, of God working in other places and, as we have seen, of the whole cosmos being brought into existence by God.

We will consider this again in chapter seven, but for now take note of how this relates to our concern in this chapter. The language about coming to God and leaving is, in Hebrew thinking, not something to be driven too far. It is parabolic, or playful, and it is this concept of playfulness which we will develop further. So it is that the writers of Psalms talk about coming to God, but they were still aware of God elsewhere. It was a way of speaking which made sense of their experience. So, if we were to use it as well, we could say that we might come to God when we shift our attention to God and pray. We will then leave again, but we trust that when we return, we will be welcomed. This is what Jesus seems to demonstrate; and this opens up to us the cycle of healing in prayer.

The Life of Christian Groups

Before we leave the subject of healing it is worth thinking briefly about how churches can, and do, operate. A church may organize itself in any number of ways but it is basically a group of people who consider themselves to be followers or disciples of Jesus. On that basis it is reasonable to expect their members to relate to each other in the kind of way that Jesus demonstrated and taught.

There is a great deal in the New Testament about how Jesus' followers should get on with each other. Some of this can be directly applied; some of it needs to be translated out of its original culture into a new situation. Churches work at this with varying degrees of success in both understanding what they are to do, and in actually doing it. One could also think about church life in terms of the way of relating that we have described as the healing cycle. We have considered how groups like families can be situations where the processes of healing are enhanced or blocked; the same is true of churches.

I have suggested that, whatever dimension of healing we are concerned with, the process will have three stages of welcome, workout and departure. I think it would help churches to ask themselves how much these are characteristics of their common life. It would also be worthwhile for someone who is considering joining a church to weigh up the extent to which the group they are thinking of joining is characterized by this process.

Like any other group, no church is going to get it right. There are, no doubt, groups of Rogerian therapists who do not treat each other with the 'unconditional positive regard' that Carl Rogers taught. There will be Transactional Analysts who will relate to each other with unhelpful Parent-Child transactions. As we have already said, this is to be expected amongst groups of people, because we are all wounded, we all carry within us a hurt Child who sometimes gets in the way of our relating to others in an appropriate Adult or Nurturing Parent mode. And no-one is exempt from the forces within and beyond us which pull us into behaviour that is destructive of our own and other people's good. Earlier theologians talked about sin being inherent within us; this is what they were talking about. And churches are not exempt from this.

Nevertheless one can still apply a critique to them. I believe churches need to think critically about themselves, so that they can become more like, or perhaps less unlike, their teacher in their behaviour. Other people need to do this if they are thinking of joining a church. It is not a matter of checking it out and deciding what a wonderful or appalling group of people a particular church is. But it is probably worthwhile someone considering whether or not a particular church is a group which will help them grow towards becoming a more whole person; whether a group which will help them live in the kind of way Jesus seems to indicate; and whether a particular church is a group in which they will be able to contribute their own insights and gifts.

Take, first of all, the welcome. There are churches where people are welcomed, accepted and valued, not necessarily by an emotional warmth as they enter the door of the worship building, but at a deeper level. The greeting counts for a lot, but a real welcome is going to give people a sense of value, and the courage to be open about themselves: how they think, or feel, what they have been through and what they have done. Some are good at this, but others can make a person feel like the woman with the haemorrhage: unclean and best out of sight.

Then there is the workout; again, in some churches there will be a real working at issues which affect their common life and their wider communities, and opportunities, whether deliberately created or naturally formed, for people to talk with each other about things that matter to them. There is also, in some churches, opportunity for people to develop their ways of praying so that these become occasions for healing and growth. But there are others where a person can feel the frustration of someone lying on a mat to whom everyone is nice and cheery, but with whom no one attempts to do anything; there is no working towards healing or movement.

Thirdly, there is the departure. Obviously people always leave their church meetings, whatever form they take. But there are some churches where no-one seems to move on, where people are thinking the same thoughts and going through the same arguments year after year. No-one seems to be taking up their mat and walking, or owning up to what they have done or what they think. But there are many where there is movement; the past is being left behind and the church is moving into new territory. A new week or a new century is seen not as a threat but as an opportunity and a gift.

In the gospel passages that we have looked at Jesus continually deals with his critics from the Adult ego-state. On some other occasions he does turn on them with aggressive condemnation, which can only be seen as him speaking as a Critical Parent. He does the same occasionally with his disciples. But, going back to our consideration of Jesus as a teacher, it seems that Jesus' preferred mode of dealing with people was as Adult-to-Adult. He gave his hearers and his critics responsibility for their decisions and their actions, and generally spoke to them in such a way that it was quite clear that he was not subservient to anyone, but neither was he out to dominate them. They could hear and they could respond; it was up to them.

This could be confirmed by reading through the gospels. In the next chapter we will turn to consider Jesus' teaching and actions with regard to violence, and here this becomes of crucial significance. But stopping for a moment longer with the matter of the type of community which encourages the process of healing, it is worth considering how important this attitude is to whether or not the healing cycle occurs.

A Question for Churches

In the gospel passages that we considered, a part of Jesus' healing work involved protecting those who needed healing from the representatives of the Law. These people – the scribes, the Pharisees, the ruler of the synagogue, and the general populace who considered the code of Law to be the definitive statement of what was acceptable to God — were all obstructing the healing process in the people who came to Jesus. And they had to be silenced before Jesus could work.

What was happening here was that the Critical Parent voices within those who needed healing were being brought out by the attitude of those around them. The question to be asked of church life is whether church members do this to each other and to those who do not belong, or whether they allow the processes of healing to work.

Jesus had to protect these people from the representatives of the Law before they could be healed. In some churches it is possible to find an attitude which is similar to that of the scribes and Pharisees. This is a stance which considers people as unacceptable until they behave better. Such an attitude will consider a person's value in terms of what they can do or have achieved. It will deem some people as in danger of contaminating the community because of who they are or what they have done. And it will adopt ways of dealing with other people which does not leave space for transactions on the Adult-to-Adult level, but will make statements which are beyond discussion and question.

In Matthew's and Luke's Gospels there is severe criticism of the scribes and the Pharisees. Bearing in mind the state of the Church when these were written it seems unlikely that the actual scribes and Pharisees were much of a danger to the churches. The Christian movement had grown rapidly and was taking a number of forms. The greater danger to the churches was people within them adopting the same attitude in the new movement as the scribes and Pharisees had taken in the old.

> *When the disciples reached the other side, they had forgotten to bring any bread. Jesus said to them, 'Watch out and beware of the yeast of the Pharisees and Saduccees'...They understood that he had not told them to beware of the yeast of the bread, but of the teaching of the Pharisees and Saduccees.*
>
> *Matthew 16:5, 6, 12*

Paul's letter to the Galatians bears this out. Here he is furious because in one of the churches he established it is now being taught, by other preachers, that the non-Jewish members need to take on board the Jewish Law. Paul's argument is not that the Law is a bad thing; he had been brought up with it and if Jewish Christians wanted to keep it that was fine by him. The danger was that people could come to believe that they were acceptable to God because of their keeping of the Law. And Paul was concerned that people should know they were accepted by God because of God's grace; in other words, that when they turned to God they were welcome.

A question therefore, for church members now, is whether they take the part of the scribes and Pharisees, or of those needing healing and of Jesus himself.

CHAPTER SIX

VIOLENCE AND JESUS' THIRD WAY

OVERVIEW

Disciples of Jesus

In chapter three we thought about two key images for our understanding of the world — firstly, that our planet is among many orbiting a star which is in turn one among millions in a universe that has been expanding for millions of years; and secondly, that life on this planet is a complex web of interconnections. The biblical writers' way of seeing the world was quite different from this but two things emerged as we brought the two into focus. One was that much that the biblical writers had to say was compatible with our own way of understanding the world, not as a scientific perspective, but as a source of wisdom concerning the value of life and of humanity's place within it. The second was that while, on the one hand, there was a view in the Bible that the world had been made and finished, there was also a sense of God being continually active within the life of the world. Taken on its own the opening chapter of Genesis, which is the most well-known passage about creation, could give an idea that God was to be thought of as having made the world back in the beginning and then left it, as a job well done. However, other poetic passages in the Bible, and particularly the psalms, give a clear sense of God being continually at work in the processes of the world.

In chapter four we considered the way that our Western sense of ourselves is not only that we decide to do things but also that we are influenced by drives and forces within and beneath our conscious minds. Bringing together this key image of ourselves with a number of episodes from the gospels we then develop another image. The picture that develops is of a possible cycle of healing in which the forces that disable people are overcome, enabling them to become more free and creative.

In the last chapter we saw how, on a number of occasions, Jesus protected people from those who would condemn them. A number of people who would be condemned to continued disability, exclusion from society or even stoning to death were healed or set free by Jesus. The custodians of the moral and religious 'law' were, in a way, pushed to one side by Jesus.

That does not mean that Jesus was not concerned with how people lived. His basic message according to Matthew's and Mark's Gospels was that people should repent, and believe the good news that the kingdom of God was near. To 'repent' is to turn around — to change one's attitude and behaviour. And, on numerous occasions, what Jesus sets out for people as a way of living is very demanding.

This is summed up in Matthew's Gospel where after a whole series of passages in which Jesus gives an alternative to the old teaching, he says, 'Be perfect ... as your heavenly Father is perfect.' *(Matthew 5:48)* The perfection he is talking about, he has already stated:

> *'You have heard that it was said, "You shall love your neighbour and hate your enemy." But I say to you, Love your enemies and pray for those who persecute you, so that you may be children of your Father in heaven; for he makes his sun rise on the evil and on the good, and sends rain on the righteous and the unrighteous.'*
>
> *(Matthew 5:43–45)*

The word 'perfect', when applied to life, often conjures up for people something very constrained and pinned down. Being perfect will sometimes be heard as meaning avoiding lots of wrong things: not doing bad things. And it has often been taught this way in Christian circles. But the perfection Jesus is talking about is not something static but dynamic. It begins with the love of God, which Jesus himself lives out in his dealings with the people who are condemned or pushed to the margins. In response to that love people should live out the same attitude.

The idea of God continually avoiding doing wrong is obviously absurd. However else God is thought of, in the traditions of the Bible God is continually creatively active. God's perfection is therefore not a matter of God not doing this or that which is wrong, but of God being God. So the perfection that Jesus is talking about is going to be a matter of people who, according to the book of Genesis, are made in the image of God, being themselves and doing what it is their thing to do. The action that Jesus calls for will also be people being true to themselves, and being creative.

Saint Paul, in his letters, realized that his argument that people are brought into a right relationship with God by God's grace rather than by ethical achievement might lead people into thinking that it did not matter what they did. In fact, they might go further and suggest that it was better to do a lot of wrong so that God could have a chance to be even more gracious and forgiving. That, said Paul, was to miss the point completely. It is not a matter of God sitting watching people's lives and keeping a score which he can then graciously wipe off from time to time, but of God actively involved in the life of the world, inviting and encouraging people to join in with what he is doing. (See *Romans 6:1–4*)

Paul's mission was to bring the gospel to Gentiles, and he argued vehemently that they did not need to take on the Jewish Law in order to be Christian. His letters invariably move from statements about the way that God works to the implications of this for the way that Christians should live. This is not a new Law but the way that life in the Spirit of God works out in communities and societies as a whole.

Matthew's Gospel came from a Christian community which kept much more to its Jewish roots. More than anyone else in the New Testament, except perhaps the writer of The Letter to the Hebrews, Matthew refers to what has been said by the prophets, to point out ways that Jesus fulfilled their expectations. And on one occasion he has Jesus say, 'The scribes and Pharisees sit on Moses' seat; therefore do whatever they teach you and follow it; but do not do as they do, for they do not practice what they teach.' (*Matthew 23:2–3*) Then follows a lengthy condemnation of the scribes and Pharisees for many of their practices and attitudes which, no doubt, Matthew saw as potentially, if not actually, present within the Church.

Returning for a moment to the image of the cycle of healing, what this clearly calls for is the person to move out of their disabled position into a new creative freedom but not to discard totally the messages that have come from the Critical Parent figures. These are now to be assessed. There may be much there that is of value and which it is good to keep. But the free person is not now to struggle to keep to the instructions in order to acquire favour or merit, but because there is sound advice or wisdom in this teaching.

With regard to the actual teaching of the scribes and Pharisees, the churches of Paul and of Matthew came to different conclusions and took a different line. It is clear from the New Testament that the earliest churches were not unanimous in how they dealt with the Law and the scribes' interpretation of it. But they were agreed on the centrality of Jesus' actions and teaching for working out how they related to God and how they were to relate to other people. The disciples of Jesus were not just those who had listened to Jesus or possibly travelled with him in Galilee and Judea, but included themselves. They were disciples in their own time and place, and encouraged others to join in taking on for themselves his teaching and way of living.

We will explore this further with regard to one significant issue for individuals and society: the matter of violence. There are many other issues we could deal with, but the aim of this book is not to try and sort everything out, even if that were possible. What I am trying to do here is to give some key images for Christian thinking and living, and violence is a good issue to focus on. One way or another, dealing with violence is a part of everyone's experience. And if we cannot work out a way of dealing creatively with our own tendencies to violence and the violence in our world, we will not survive. On that basis alone the possibilities that Jesus puts forward must be worth considering. It also happens that the way that Jesus approaches the whole matter of violence is a good demonstration of the way that he teaches a dynamic rather than a static approach to life.

The Fight–Flight Response

One of the curses of Western society at the present time is stress-related disease. Stress itself is not a problem; without some stress we do not get on and do things. In order to rise to challenges and carry out tasks, everyone needs a certain degree of stress. Without it we are like untuned guitar strings which just flop around with a dull thump. Stress is the body's response to threat. When something happens which threatens us there is a charge of adrenaline within our bodies, our heart rate increases and our senses become more highly tuned to be able to move quickly. This is sometimes known as the fight–flight response.

It is built into us as animals and without it we could not survive. A stone age man is going through the forest and meets a sabre-toothed tiger. Suddenly there is a flood of adrenaline for him to either fight it, or to run. Whichever way he chooses he needs the supercharge to help him do it. Once he has fought the animal, and survived, or run away and escaped, his body settles down to its normal state, until the next time. Without that fight–flight response our ancestors would never have made it through the forests.

One difficulty in our society is that our organization and lifestyle is such that often there is a series of challenges but no way of burning off the adrenaline boost. Driving a car along a motorway is a situation of great danger. Drivers get used to it, but even so, a few small errors on the part of another driver and our pulses are racing. We need all the quick response and fine tuning that our bodies can give us to get along the tarmac at seventy miles an hour and survive.

But what do we actually do? The physical activity involved is negligible. There is no way of burning off the adrenaline in a car. We are just sitting there, moving our feet and hands. And once we arrive at the other end there is probably another chair to sit on, and people who need to be spoken to calmly and coolly, regardless of what we really feel about them and the experience we have just had on the road.

The sabre-toothed tiger in the forest, or the thirty-ton truck changing lane on the motorway, are both obvious threats to our survival. Others are less obvious, but the possible failure in a piece of work which can threaten our future employment, loss of respect from a colleague, or departure of a friend or partner, are also threats to us, in a different kind of way.

The everyday dealings we have with people are also loaded with significance for us. We often do not recognize it, but sometimes the statements and gestures of other people come through to us with the added force of our accumulated memories. Things said and done to us by people when we are adults can stir in us all sorts of memories of when we were not adults, but small and weak and needing help and care, when we were children.

And we are often dealing with many different threats without having the time to assimilate one before the next arrives. Our bodies can spend long periods tuned up for dealing with threats but have little opportunity for tuning down. There are not enough situations for our bodies to return to a restful state, and perhaps there are too many threats. The result is like a build up of energy which needs some kind of outlet. The question is, what do we do with the energy?

It might be internalized, producing mental or even physical behaviour which is self-destructive; it might suddenly burst out in rage or explosive violence; it might be dissipated slowly over a period of time; we might release it in some burst of physical activity. There are a number of ways people deliberately or unconsciously develop to expend the energy that builds up as a result of the fight-flight response. Not everyone suffers from a stress-related disease, though many do, but it may be that some who do not are involved in causing it in others. The explosive violence in which a person dissipates their own burst of energy is usually destructive of things or of other people. So it is not just a matter of getting rid of the energy. It is a matter of letting this natural fight–flight response become something constructive or creative, of finding an alternative to violence.

Forms of Threat and Violence

When we are threatened we have a boost of energy, brought about in us by a surge of adrenaline. What do we do with that energy? In its simplest form that question is presented to us when we are faced with someone who is going to hit us. Do we take evasive action, let them do it, hit them back afterwards, or make a pre-emptive strike? This dilemma is often broken down into two possibilities: we either use violence in response, or we do not. If we do not use violence in response and we cannot get away, we get hit. We will return to this dilemma shortly, but first we need to consider some of the ways that this issue presents itself. They are not always immediately obvious.

In the ninth century a large part of Britain was invaded by Vikings. Their view was simple; they would fight the people who were there, and if they won then they would take over their land. They would have said there was nothing wrong with that; they might argue that victory showed the gods were on their side or they might just say that that was how the world was, and it was up to the inhabitants to defend themselves. This approach to life was not original, nor were they the last people to take it. Three thousand years ago the empires of the Middle East were rising and collapsing in wave after wave of conflict and conquest. Hidden from the view of the big powers, the Hebrews took over the land of the Canaanites, claiming that Yahweh was on their side giving them the victory. A thousand years after the Vikings invaded Britain, Europeans were taking over America, Australasia and Africa with the same kind of justification.

This kind of approach to life might now be disparaged in Europe and America, and one task of the United Nations is to try to stop it. However the same approach can be taken in economics and be widely accepted. It is a commonly held belief that if I have the money to pay for something I have the right to own it, regardless of whether someone else needs it more. It is up to them to come up with the money for the goods. One might call this 'economic violence'.

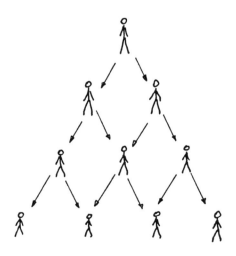

In the previous chapter we saw that one possible response to being 'put down' by a person who is adopting the Critical Parent attitude towards us, is to adopt the same attitude towards them, and try to 'get one over on them'. This can then make the situation escalate.

Each time one person is trying to 'get on top of' the other, and what might start with words can end in physical violence, as the adrenaline charges continue and the people concerned become more and more geared to action. This kind of relationship can build up into a whole structure of people getting themselves 'on top of' others, in order to respond to what they perceive as threats. Put diagrammatically this would come out as a pyramid.

It is interesting the way that the phrases 'on top of', and 'get one over on' give a sense of conflict: one trying to get into a position of strength with regard to the other, like two animals fighting. With more sophisticated words, like 'superiority', the same sense is there. The diagrams almost draw themselves.

The similarity between this kind of picture and a diagram of a military command system or the management of many large corporations is not a coincidence. What we have there is a social structure which is formalized so that people know their place — who they are superior to, and who is below them. This can provide ease of communication, and a sense of security, and does not necessarily involve violence, but it can do. In some less formalized structures, like city gangs or the Mafia, the organization is held in place by threats, if not by actual violence. Threats of various kinds might also hold other more socially acceptable organizations in place.

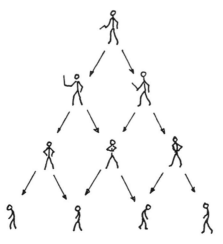

One could consider this use of threats as a form of violence. During the apartheid years in South Africa very often the police and military used physical violence to keep the black people in the places allotted to them, and to break up protests. Many suggested that the threat of violence, the verbal abuse, and the system of checks and passes, were also forms of violence. The freedom and dignity of the black people was being violated.

In a multitude of other ways, people's dignity as individuals of value is violated the world over. This happens physically in racial attacks and rapes, muggings and child abuse. It happens in more subtle ways when those with power devise or enforce laws which give some people less respect than they consider to be due to themselves. In thinking about violence we are thinking about more than simple physical attack and defence. But if we can work out a good way to handle that simple kind of situation we may then have a clue towards working out good ways of dealing with other forms of violence. The creative response to a simple threat can become a key image for handling more subtle, or more complex, forms of violence.

Jesus' Teaching and Response to Violence

The clearest and most well known statement of Jesus on violence is in Matthew's Gospel:

> *Jesus said, 'You have heard that it was said, "An eye*
> *for an eye and a tooth for a tooth."*
> *But I say to you, do not resist an evildoer.*
> *But if anyone strikes you on the right cheek, turn the*
> *other also; and if anyone wants to sue you and take*
> *your coat, give your cloak as well; and if anyone*
> *forces you to go one mile, go also the second mile.*
> *Give to everyone who begs from you,*
> *and do not refuse anyone who wants*
> *to borrow from you.'*
>
> (Matthew 5:38–42)

This is often taken to mean that Jesus was advocating making no response to violence, but that the appropriate thing to do was to just let the perpetrator carry on. For centuries that has been a widely held view of what Jesus meant. It has also been generally ignored by Christians. They have not only fought in wars but also perpetrated crusades. These things have been justified on the basis that Jesus' teaching here was totally unrealistic, or only need be applied to special individuals like monks and clergy. The ordinary Christian could ignore this 'counsel of perfection', as it was called.

But reading this as advocating no response to violence ignores the detail of the text, and the setting in which it came. Resistance had the same ring for people in Jesus' society as it had for people in Europe in the 1940s and 1950s. It meant armed resistance, violent defence or insurrection, or taking up battle positions. Paul uses the word in his letter to Ephesians when he speaks of the Christian as having the armour of God to withstand the assaults of the power of evil.

• *The right cheek*

In his simple example Jesus actually specifies the *right* cheek. If someone hits you on the right cheek, says Jesus, offer him the other as well. Jesus lived in a totally right-handed society. As in much of the Middle East and Africa today the left hand was only used for dirty jobs. Hitting was always done with the right hand. If it was a direct assault it was with the fist. If the hit was an insult, a slap, it was done with the back of the hand. That was how centurions hit legionaries, masters hit slaves, and men hit women. The only way you can hit someone's right cheek with your right hand is with the back of it. This was not an assault, it was an insult. In that situation, says Jesus, offer him the other cheek. Do not accept the insult but challenge your assailant to hit you like an equal.

• *The coat and the cloak*

The situation of the coat and the cloak is similar. People only wore two garments: an under garment, called a *chiton,* and an outer garment, called a *himation.* The situation here is that someone who is in debt has been taken to court for repayment. The repayment of debts features quite often in the teaching and parables of Jesus. It was a common problem as poor people struggled to survive and the rich wanted to increase their security by taking over more land. The man being sued is being squeezed to his last garment. Jesus' suggestion is to take off the other one and give him the lot.

For us that presents a comic situation and there and then it would have raised some laughs as well, but with an added sting. The man doing the suing, like everyone else, was concerned about his dignity.

In the case of a man standing naked in that society there was not so much shame on the naked man as on those who saw him naked. The man who was doing the suing would not only be embarrassed and made a laughing stock with a story that would run like wildfire round the villages, but he would also be shamed before the magistrate and others whose opinion of him mattered.

• *The extra mile*

It would be a Roman soldier who might force someone to go one mile. The Roman military had the authority on occasion to requisition assistance when they were on the march. But there were strict controls over what they could requisition. The authorities were concerned to keep the peace and not stir up rebellion so whilst soldiers could sometimes force people to carry their packs, they could only do so for one mile. Then they must take the pack back. The word used here is the word used in the regulations about requisitioning.

What Jesus suggests here is that the person with the pack should carry on. Suddenly the legionary is caught out; he needs his pack back. He must have his pack back, otherwise he can be severely flogged for having made a civilian go too far. So what does he do? Does he plead with this Jew to give him back his pack and endure ridicule from passers-by? Does he try not to make a fuss and risk serious trouble? He is in a situation he has not been in before; he is no longer in charge of the situation and no longer in the dominant position.

• *Give and survive*

Then Jesus says to give to the one who asks something of you. He might be a beggar or he might be a neighbour who needs a loan and either asks you, his friend, or falls into the hands of the loan sharks. Jesus was talking to the poor, to peasants struggling to get by. This was a simple matter of struggling to get by together.

• *Challenging violence*

This teaching about violence is contained in Luke's Gospel as well (*Luke 6:27–31*). Some of the detail is different but the sense is the same. Here it is framed by two other sentences which give the basic idea of what Jesus was talking about: 'I say to you listen, love your enemies, do good to those who hate you, bless those who curse you, pray for those who abuse you.'

See the other person as a person, and do good to them. Do not make them objects of hatred, to be destroyed or removed, but treat them as people. To love enemies does not mean to feel good about them, nor to do whatever they want; it means to stretch oneself to do what is best for them. This will often mean challenging them, but doing it Adult to Adult. 'Do to others as you would have them do to you.' (*Matthew 7:12.*)

This theme is taken up by Paul in his letters. 'See that none of you repays evil for evil, but always seek to do good to one another and to all.' (*1 Thessalonians 5:15 . See also: Romans 12:17–21 and 1 Peter 3:9*). The challenge is to reply to the clear or subtle violence or some other destructive action, not with more of the same, but with a creative response. This is a third way of responding to violence. It is by neither fighting back, nor just letting it happen, but doing something else which respects the other person and challenges them to give you the respect you are due.

There is a difficulty with words here. The word that is sometimes used for this is 'non-violence', but that is inadequate. The very word 'non-violence' turns us back to this idea of the right thing being the avoidance of wrong. But it is not a matter of avoiding wrong, but of something much more imaginative and exciting, and powerful. This is neither violence nor an avoidance of violence, but a third approach.

Creativity is a key component of this response to violence that Jesus calls for. Part of its power is the element of surprise for the one who threatens. The soldier who must argue for his pack has not imagined this happening. The one demanding the cloak has not anticipated being shamed in the lawcourt by his impoverished debtor stripping off.

These sayings of Jesus are not laws. They are examples of a kind of response which is in tune with the creative love of God for both the perpetrator and oneself. They are challenges which respect the perpetrator of the violence, and at the same time do not deny one's own worth, whilst creating a new situation.

Characteristics of the Creative Response

This kind of approach has been developed with considerable effect in recent decades. Gandhi, influenced greatly by his reading of the gospels, taught and used it in India, as did Martin Luther King in the USA. It was practised extensively against the apartheid regime in South

Africa and by Solidarity in Poland, and other movements in Eastern Europe. There are movements of resistance to South American dictatorships who practice this approach, as well as environmental campaign groups all over the world.

Jesus gave a summary statement of this kind of approach, and some examples of what it would mean. This approach has been used and developed in a multitude of different situations, and out of this have come what might be described as guidelines or ground-rules. The American writer, Walter Wink, from his work in the USA and South Africa has set these out as follows:

- *Seize the moral initiative*
- *Find a creative alternative to violence*
- *Assert your own humanity and dignity as a person*
- *Meet force with ridicule or humour*
- *Break the cycle of humiliation*
- *Refuse to submit to or accept the inferior position*
- *Expose the injustice of the system*
- *Take control of the power dynamic*
- *Shame the oppressor into repentance*
- *Stand your ground*
- *Make the Powers make decisions for which they are not prepared*
- *Recognize your own power*
- *Be willing to suffer rather than retaliate*
- *Force the oppressor to see you in a new light*
- *Deprive the oppressor of a situation where a show of force is effective*
- *Be willing to undergo the penalty of breaking unjust laws*
- *Die to fear of the old order and its rules*
- *Seek the oppressor's transformation*

(Walter Wink, *Engaging the Powers* [1])

Despite the Church's collusion with aggression and oppression down the centuries, and its support of war on occasions, it is worth bearing in mind that in the first few centuries, Christians did not join the armed forces and were seen as a threat to the Roman power. They were persecuted as a threat, not because they were trying to take over control of the empire, but because they threatened its whole culture and organization of violence. They were a counter-culture, not abiding by the rules that others took for granted as being the way of the world.

Using the Energy

This way of responding to overt or institutional violence will not be easy. It can be thought of as a third way because it is neither fighting back with the same techniques and violence, nor is it running away or just accepting the violence and injustice.

Such an approach will demand imagination and creativity. Jesus in Matthew's Gospel gives some examples. To make those rules would be to remove their effect. It would be the element of surprise which would catch the Roman soldier or the demanding moneylender off guard. New creative responses would be needed continually, and creativity often needs humour. That can be hard under pressure, and in the face of challenge. It can also be painful and risky. It is never clear how the aggressor will respond to the creative challenge. Gandhi insisted that only people who would be willing to fight for independence could join him. This way was no easy option. Jesus said to a great crowd that was following him: 'If any want to become my followers, let them deny themselves and take up their cross and follow me.' *(Mark 8:34).* Here again this warning also indicates something of the process. The cross was not something that people took up, it was something that was put on the back of a convicted rebel and to which the rebel was nailed. Jesus says his followers must take the initiative, and pick up the cross.

The difficulty of this approach does answer the question of what one does with the energy that comes in response to the threat. The energy may be a sudden charge in response to immediate danger, or a slow seething anger in the face of consistent abuse and injustice. The answer is to channel that energy into a creative challenge to the perpetrator.

That then raises another question: how does one channel the energy? A short answer is that it will take practice, and people can help each other to do it. This is why people actively trying to encourage this approach will not just talk about it but develop training, and encourage people to work together.

But there are other things that can be said from the teaching and life of Jesus, which are relevant and which may be helpful. The first is, as we saw in the previous chapter, that Jesus valued, and taught that God values, the powerless as well as the powerful. One effect of violence or oppression is that those who suffer come to feel that they are of little or no value. But if someone can hold on to the fact that they are of value to God, as much value as anyone else, they might have strength to resist. This is how it was that people were able to resist apartheid and segregation persistently over decades; they believed they mattered to God as much as those who had the political power.

On its own, this sense of one's own worth could lead to a struggle to reverse roles, or a tendency to respond with similar violence. What is needed to correct this is a sense that the other person, however aggressive, violent, unjust or oppressive they are, is still a person who matters. Often this person's violence will come from a lack of self-worth, as they might be caught up in a whole system of oppression and degradation. Or, with an individual acting alone, it might arise from a sense of worthlessness brought about by severe mistreatment or neglect when they were young. This is not necessarily the case, but it is always a possibility to be considered.

It is said that Leonard Wilson, later a Bishop of Birmingham, was interred when the Japanese overran Singapore during the Second World War. He and his companion in prison were regularly beaten by the prison officers. After one bout Wilson's companion thanked God that the beating was over. Wilson replied that he thanked God that he could still love the prison officers. His companion asked in amazement how he could do that. Wilson's answer was that he imagined what they might have been like as children.

A belief that the perpetrator of the violence is also valuable to God might provide a basis for developing responses which give the perpetrator a respect which they are not giving to their victim. But holding to that will be part of the mental struggle of responding to violence with Jesus' third method; this will call for imagination and creative reflection. Martin Luther King's persistent work for civil rights in America was intimately connected with his theological thinking, his preaching and his praying. And Gandhi drew the strength he needed from meditation. We will return to consider these kind of activities in the next chapter, but one other significant feature of Jesus' life and teaching needs to be considered: that is, that Jesus taught that the kingdom of God was breaking in through what he was doing. The phrase, kingdom of God, perhaps seems remote and otherworldly, but it is intimately connected with what we are considering here.

God's New Order

Jesus was called the Messiah on occasions. This was the old Hebrew term for God's chosen king. Literally it means 'Yahweh's anointed'. The ritual of kingmaking in ancient Israel involved the pouring of oil or ointment onto the head of the new monarch. Someone anointed by Yahweh was not only the people's king but also Yahweh God's king. At the time of the Roman occupation of Palestine expectations were high that God would send a new Messiah to liberate the people and establish God's reign.

Jesus was not happy with the title, for many people had in their minds a clear idea of what the Messiah would do. The Messiah would raise an army and lead a successful rebellion against the Romans, and establish the reign of God. Many expected that the Messiah would fight violence with violence, and win. That was not Jesus' programme. However Jesus did preach that the reign of God was close by. The kingdom of God was at hand. Tax collectors and prostitutes were going into the kingdom before the scribes and Pharisees. The kingdom was there, among them, or within them.

Jesus' parables were frequently about the kingdom, or reign, of God: it was growing like a seed; it was unseen like yeast in a lump of dough; it was worth giving up a great deal for, in the way that a dealer sells all his pearls for one of extreme value or a man sells everything he has in order to buy a field where he knows there is buried treasure.

Jesus clearly saw the reign of God as something which was breaking into the world, or growing within it. In the Old Testament God was fundamentally the Creator, who worked imaginatively to bring the world into being, to sustain it and repair it, and to bring people into a new relationship with himself. The coming of the reign of God can therefore be seen as another part of God's whole creative work. It can be seen as a new order of relationship between people, and between people and God the Creator.

In Jesus' view this new order was not characterized by violence. That was the hallmark of the old order of Rome, Persia, Assyria, Babylon, Egypt, and all the warring tribes of the world. It was also the hallmark of those who threw their weight around, who used their money and power to gain more at the expense of those with greater need. It was characteristic of those who used their status in society as men, or as adults, or as good and honourable people, to push down those who had less influence. God's reign was characterized by another kind of relationship, which acknowledged that all humanity, and not only a part of humanity, was created in the image of God.

Jesus' Challenge to the Old Order

After working in Galilee Jesus went to Jerusalem and staged a deliberate demonstration there. He timed his arrival to coincide with the excitement of the Passover festival and the arrival of thousands of pilgrims from Galilee and elsewhere. He rode into the city on a donkey, a traditional mark of a king arriving in peace, and he staged a demonstration in the Court of Gentiles in the temple, throwing out the moneychangers and dealers there. Then he taught each day in the temple and waited for the authorities to respond.

If Jesus had raised an army they might have known what to do. It would not have been the first time that had happened; it was the usual course for any prospective Messiah. If Jesus had gone back to Galilee, or shown any sign of subservience in the face of their questioning and challenges, they might have found a way to tolerate or patronize him. If he had tried to justify his teaching about God valuing the social rejects as much as the respectable people they could have argued with him. But he did none of those things. He tossed back their challenges, and criticized the scribes and Pharisees to the crowds.

Their final response was arrest and an irregular trial. He was taken to Pilate, the Governor, and questioned. His answers were few, and simply affirming a few of the statements that they themselves had made. He did not argue or threaten, or plead. He simply stood there in front of them. Only when he was crucified did the cool resolve break. According to Matthew and Mark he shouted in puzzled anger at being left by God. According to Luke he prayed that those carrying out his execution should be forgiven and commended his spirit to God, whom he addressed as Father. But there is no report that he cursed or pleaded with his torturers as he died. Right through to the end he maintained the same approach. He presented a peaceful challenge to those in power. The way that Jesus taught for responding to violence was Jesus' own continual attitude, right until his death.

The conviction of his disciples after some days was that Jesus' death was not the end, but that God had carried out a new act of creativity. Jesus, they said, was raised from the dead. He was risen, alive with the life of God. And far from being a failed messiah, as they and the authorities had thought, he was *the* Messiah. He had been true to the way of God right to the end. He had been thought to have failed because people were mistaken about how God works. The way of God was not domination and violence but new creative acts arising from a concern for the integrity and good of his creation.

It is hard to understand, from the gospel narratives, what the disciples actually experienced after Jesus' crucifixion. There are various stories which include the discovery of an empty tomb, the activity of angels, and Jesus meeting with them in bodily form but not confined by doors and walls. It was, in these appearances, the same body. Jesus had the marks of the crucifixion, but he was not a resuscitated corpse. These appearances are few, and then they cease. From then on the disciples continue to speak of Christ as alive but in two kinds of ways: Jesus was alive in the realm of God, and also active in the world by his Spirit.

We move then into the difficult realm of trying to make sense of what they found difficult to describe. We will return to this whole business of the Spirit in the next chapter. With regard to the whole matter of responding to violence, the point is that Jesus' first disciples were convinced that his approach was right, even after they had seen him crucified. And they were convinced that the real power lay in his hands, not in those of Pilate and the Jewish authorities, with all their ability to threaten, and to carry out, violence.

Moreover they had seen Jesus crucified, or at least been told what had happened. According to Mark and Matthew, people had heard him shout out, 'My God, why have you forsaken me?' They had seen him die. But that was not the end. The injustice of the trial and crucifixion and the death of Jesus were not the end of things. The Creator God had continued to be there, and had brought out of it new life and possibilities.

This has been an encouragement to people in many desperate situations: a continual reminder that violence and injustice do not have the last word; and that even in a situation of apparent dereliction the creator God is still present and active. For some in their own isolation and pain there has been a sense that, though alone, they are suffering with a multitude of others down history and across the world; and in the midst is the young man on a cross crying out to the God he believes has left him. That has given them strength and courage to stay with it and to hope, even against the odds and when they cannot imagine a future different from the present.

Grace, and the Mess of the World

Sometimes perhaps it seems that this approach will not work; however hard one looks one cannot see how a creative challenge can achieve anything. In this situation one might say that the consequences of the crucifixion could not be foreseen either — we cannot see or imagine all possibilities.

But there are possibly situations where, to do anything other than use violence, is to allow worse consequences. One can think of the need to forcibly restrain a person who is doing serious harm to someone who is unable to respond: the disturbed gunman shooting at children; the paranoid dictator with weapons of mass destruction at his disposal. These are the stuff of which bad dreams are made, but they are also sometimes a part of the real world. These situations present something like Bonhoeffer's dilemma.

Dietrich Bonhoeffer was a pastor in the German Church at the time of Hitler's rise to power. He believed that the use of violence was wrong, and used his abilities to broadcast, preach, argue and organize, to resist the Nazis. Eventually he came to believe that non-violence would not work in stopping the evil that the Nazis were perpetrating. He then engaged in deceit, pretending to work for the government while using the opportunity to travel and to maintain contacts with other churches abroad, and he became involved in a plot to assassinate Hitler. He was finally arrested, and executed a month before the end of the Second World War.

To the end Bonhoeffer did not try to argue that he was doing right in plotting to kill Hitler. It was wrong, but the alternatives were worse. The fact was, as he saw it, that the world was a mess, and sometimes decisions are not between a right and a wrong but between two courses of action both of which are wrong. In that situation the Christian must not avoid making a decision, nor justify his actions. The Christian must act and take responsibility for doing wrong, trusting ultimately in the mercy, or grace, of God.

Saint Paul called Jesus the image of the invisible God. Presented with hard choices perhaps many of us have a tendency, if we think about God at all, to imagine God as the fearful judge: the Critical Parent writ large. The attitude of Jesus to the woman with the haemorrhage, or the man paralysed by his sense of failure, or the woman caught having sex with a man who was not her prospective husband, was different. With these encounters in mind we can perhaps alter our picture, and feel less that there is a need to get it right than there is an opportunity to do something new and creative.

With this in mind we can also address the more subtle issues of economic and structural violence, of destructive relationships and the sense of threat and fear which can easily diminish the lives of the people we work with, as well as ourselves. In doing so we could turn to other aspects of Jesus' teaching and other features of his attitude to life which might throw light on both the situation and on the creative possibilities for us.

But in this book, we will move on. We will now turn to consider play and the life of the Spirit, and what might help us develop the combination of playfulness, imagination and creativity that we need to live in the way of God in a violent and messy world.

1   Walter Wink, *Engaging the Powers* (Augsburg Fortress, 1992) p. 186f. Reprinted by permission from *Engaging The Powers* by Walter Wink, copyright © 1992 Augsburg Fortress.

CHAPTER SEVEN

PLAY AND THE LIFE OF THE SPIRIT

OVERVIEW

A Problem with Words

There have been forms of Christianity which have reduced the whole thing to following the teaching and example of the man from Galilee. But a question that arises from this is the one that arose in the last chapter: what can help us develop the creativity, imagination and play-fulness which we need to live in the way that Jesus taught and showed? We could also ask what resources are available to help us live with a continuing concern for other people and the world.

Clearly, for the first Christians the movement was not just a com-mitment to the teaching and example of Jesus although this was cer-tainly important to them. If it had not been they would not have both-ered to write and preserve the gospels. What Jesus said and did, and what happened to him, were clearly of crucial importance to the movement in the early days. But the early writings, and particularly the letters of Paul and The Acts of the Apostles also have a considerable amount to say about the 'Spirit'.

There are other forms of Christianity which emphasize the 'Spirit' a great deal, but here two other problems can emerge. It does not necessarily happen but one can find Christian groups who talk a great deal about the 'Spirit' but seem to have little concern for the teaching and life of Jesus. These may be highly institutional churches or loose knit groups, but churches are certainly around whose interest in Jesus himself stretches little beyond a statement that he died and rose again. This is not a recent phenomenon. It is noticeable that some of the earliest statements of Christian belief, like the Apostles' Creed, say nothing about Jesus between him being 'born of the Virgin Mary' and having 'suffered under Pontius Pilate'. The question that arises here is simply, why do the gospels say so much more if it is of such little importance? It was clearly not unimportant to the first followers of Jesus.

The second problem that sometimes emerges with groups that emphasize the 'Spirit' is that experiences of the 'Spirit' are identified with the weird and strange, or with particular emotions. When this happens talk about the 'Spirit' breaks away from its Hebrew roots in which the Spirit is God active in creation. Instead of being seen as the dynamism of life the Spirit is thought of as a supernatural power.

We will return shortly to thinking more about the term 'spirit' which was a key image for the thinking of the first Christians, but we will start by considering two features of life as most people experience it. At some time or other play is a part of everyone's experience. A sense of wonder is likewise something that seems to take hold of most people at some moments in their lives. We will begin with these phenomena.

There is a story told about a pious lady whose house was caught up in a flood. When the water was up to her doorstep rescue workers came by with a boat. She refused to get in. 'The Lord will save me,' she said. They went on and rescued other people.

Later the water had reached the upstairs. Another boat came by. 'The Lord will save me,' she said, and refused to get in.

The water rose up to the roof and she was clinging on to the chimney. A helicopter came over and a man was winched down to pick her up. She refused to go. 'The Lord will save me!' she cried. The water rose further, over the house, and the lady drowned.

She arrived in heaven and said to the Lord angrily, 'I trusted in you. Why didn't you save me?' The Lord answered, 'I sent you boats and a helicopter. What more did you expect?' [1]

It would be possible to tell that story in some circles and not raise a laugh or a smile, if the hearers have that woman's kind of piety, or they think that jokes involving God are in bad taste. It could be that for some reason they just would not see the joke, in which case to try to explain it would be hopeless. One could point out what was happening in the story; but when explained, no joke is funny. You either get it or you do not.

Wonder is a similar experience. It is possible for someone to go out on a sunny day and be struck by the blueness of the sky. They know that the sky is blue, when it is not white or grey and raining, but on this occasion the blueness is striking. They see it contrasted against the green of a tree, and it is almost as if they have never seen its blueness before. For a moment it holds their attention, without thoughts about the refraction of light through the atmosphere or the prospects of it holding out till the weekend. They simply wonder at the blueness.

But it is then hard to explain that to someone else. They get back into the office and say, 'At lunchtime I noticed the sky was blue.' What happens? They receive a round of applause perhaps. People wonder if such an 'immature' person ought to be doing that job. Someone thinks this is another conversation about the weather. They can perhaps try to explain about their experience, but even if they took the others outside they would have great difficulty getting other people from the office to enter into that experience. The only way they might manage it is by being poetic, and trying to catch somebody into the experience.

The same thing can happen on a Monday morning. At the weekend someone went to a jazz club. They were caught up in it: the movement of the sounds, the pleasure, the laughter, the whole life of the place. On Monday they try to tell their colleagues.

'We had a great time.'

'What happened?'

'Well, this band played. They were good. And we had a few drinks. It was fantastic!'

'Great. Well, about this sales schedule...'

You either get it or you don't. You cannot have it second hand.

Play

Play is very similar. Children are good at it; they just let go and play. As long as they are feeling reasonably secure you can say to children, 'Go off and play,' and they will. They get into playing like diving into a swimming pool. Adults, at least in Western society, generally find it harder.

Play is a whole mêlée of activities. It usually involves pleasure, fun, enjoyment, and maybe laughter. There is a letting go and getting involved. It might be tiring but it is also relaxing. Play might be energetic, but it is also energizing. There is perhaps an outcome, but that cannot be taken too seriously. If the result of the football match is too important it stops being a game.

A person gets involved in play, and loses self-consciousness. If a child becomes aware that people think they are daft dressed up like an alien, or a man begins to feel childish lying on the floor making a noise like a grizzly bear, he ceases for a moment to play. Perhaps, with an act of will, and a letting go of these concerns, the person can enter back into the game.

Play is also likely to involve imagination, and be creative. A game might have rules, but within that frame there is no proper way to play it; there might be good ways and bad ways. There may be ways that spoil the game for others or that damage the equipment, but there are not proper ways of playing it. Imagine a boy given a Lego set for Christmas. He unwraps it and then his father begins to show him the proper way to make a zyphon-ray space-mobile. The boy does not want to do it the proper way; he wants to play with it. He might copy what is in the diagram but if he does, it is because he chooses to.

Play can take place where there is security; a person who is anxious or frightened cannot play spontaneously. They might, by an act of will, png to take their mind of   f the threat or danger, like the person in the hospital waiting room who plays Solitaire. This is then a mental act which focuses the mind away from the cause of worry. They might then, for a few moments, be able to play. There might then be some fun in it, but they have to work their way into it.

Entertainers are nervous before going on stage. They have their opening lines ready, and from practice can switch on the smile and the laugh. Once they have developed a rapport with the audience they can begin to play, and the wit and humour can become spontaneous.

Similarly, if a person has a sense of guilt or serious unease about what they are doing it is hard for them to play until they have suppressed or worked out that feeling. If a preacher tells a joke at the beginning of a sermon and from the response picks up that this has caused offence or upset, it is hard for him to be light or humorous in what he is saying.

A person who could never be serious would have difficulty in relating to others, and in carrying out the basic tasks that living requires. Similarly it would be difficult to live with someone who never played, who had no sense of humour, and for whom everything was hard work. In both cases others would tend to think there was something wrong with the person. Play seems to be something which mentally healthy people do sometimes.

A young child in a playground will return periodically to a parent or carer. After having a moment's attention the child will then go off and play for a while. The older the child is, generally, the longer the child will play without having to return to the adult. An anxious or ill child will return more often, or even be unwilling to go away. Eventually the child goes to school for long periods of the day, and finally, in the usual run of things, leaves home.

Adults also operate in cycles. A person who spends long periods of time assessing information and making decisions, operating in the Adult or Parent ego-state, occasionally needs to move into the Child mode. They may do that by reading a book, playing a game, with their children or friends, they may do it in bed with their lover, if they are not thinking about their performance, but simply playing. The adult cannot stay in this Child mode, but if the person cannot get into it at all then they are likely to have problems. The cycle is necessary for health, poise, and balance.

Neurological research in the last three decades has shown that different parts of the brain have different functions. Amongst right-handed people the creative and imaginative functions are located on the right side of the brain, whilst the logical and analytical functions are on the left side. Amongst left-handed people the reverse is true. When a right-handed person is painting, making music, writing poetry, dancing, or dreaming up possibilities for the summer holidays, they are using the right side of their brain. When they are doing their accounts, working out a train timetable, arguing with a political canvasser or working out the ingredients for the Christmas cake, they are using the left side of their brain.

People have obvious preferences and strengths. Some are cut out to be accountants, and others to be entertainers. Most people do not have a clear idea of being cut out for anything in particular and end up doing all sorts of things, but they develop different interests and hobbies. For many people play is an activity when they are using different functions from those which they use in their work — a company buyer who plays golf, a housewife who does crosswords, a vicar who reads books about trains, and a lorry driver who grows vegetables — are all, in their leisure, using different brain functions and largely using different sides of their brains. They do not think about it like that, any more than the school teacher who reads spy novels is regressing to childhood for a few minutes. They do it because it seems natural, fun, and relaxing. Looked at analytically they can be seen to be restoring a balance within themselves, by switching off some activities and switching on others for a period of time.

Symbols, Signs and the Spirit

We have already thought briefly in chapter three about the term 'spirit' in the Bible. The word is used in English translations for a Hebrew and a Greek word which can be, and sometimes is, also translated 'wind', or 'breath'. It may be that at some early time the wind was thought of as the breath of God, and the breath of a person as being their life. If that was the case, as time went on the Hebrew use of language and imagery certainly became more sophisticated, and the wind became symbolic of the life of God, and breath became symbolic of the life of the person.

The words 'sign' and 'symbol' are sometimes used to mean much the same thing and in some contexts they could be interchanged. However, in thinking about the use of visual images it is often helpful to distinguish between images which are linked with what they represent as a matter of convention or simple logic, and those which have a deeper connection. In this case the word 'symbol' is often applied to those images which have the more power and significance. The others are then often referred to as 'signs'. A sign then conveys information like the number thirty on a board beside a road, which tells drivers that they are to keep their speed down to thirty miles per hour. There is nothing significant about the shape of those numbers. It is a matter of convention. But on the corner there might be a stone cross with names inscribed on it and to the local community that war memorial could be symbolic.

The difference would be noticed if they were defaced. An aerosol spray over the road sign might cause comments of disgust at the loutish behaviour and the tax payers' money to replace it, but beyond that there would be little concern. But if the war memorial was defaced with paint it would be felt more deeply. Discussions would refer to the cross, the names of the dead who fought for their freedom, the memorial being at the centre of what was once the village and it being a part of local history.

A symbol operates on a deeper or a broader level than a sign, and draws out of the conscious or unconscious memory some kind of power by association — bread, wedding dresses, top hats, rings, flowing streams, tartan, church towers, castles, swastikas, crosses, all these could be symbolic. Signs on the other hand have a linear kind of connection with what they represent. They have meaning because the meaning has been learnt — numbers, road signs, bus stops, name badges, timetables, car park signs, pub signs. There is not much emotion involved with a sign, but there could be with a symbol. A sign is likely to draw a response from the left brain of the person and a symbol from the right. Sometimes, of course, there is a deliberate attempt to use as a sign something which is symbolic, as when as an agency works on a new company logo or a theme for a new television advert.

The wind was symbolic of the life of God, and the breath of the person was symbolic of their life. The same word was used, and the wind itself pointed to the activity of God in the world — unseen, changing, gentle or powerful, continuous. It perhaps takes imagination for us to get into that way of experiencing the world.

On occasions it is hard for a translator to know which word to use in English because it could be either 'wind' or 'spirit', as in Psalm 104 or the opening verse of Genesis. Is it spirit that God gives again to creatures on the earth, or is it breath? Is it the Spirit of God moving over the waters, or a mighty wind? The prophet Ezekiel in a great vision saw a valley of bones which came together to form corpses, but only when the wind blew down the valley did they have life and stand up as a great army.

The scholarly Nicodemus came to Jesus and Jesus told him that in order to see the kingdom of God a person had to be born again, or from above. Nicodemus did not hear this as a parable, and like someone who misses a joke, it seemed absurd. Jesus tried again: 'What is born of the flesh is flesh. What is born of the wind (spirit) is wind (spirit). The wind (spirit) blows where it will. You hear the sound of it but you do not know where it is coming from or where it is going. So it is with everyone who is born of the wind (spirit)'. *(John 3:6,8)* Any translator will opt for the word 'wind' at some points in this passage, and 'spirit' at others. That is the only way to make sense of it in English. But Jesus here is playing with the word in a short parable about the way that those who see the kingdom are those who are tuned into life.

The Activity of the Spirit

Like trying to catch the wind in a bag it is impossible to pin down how, in the Bible, the spirit actually works. Consider a selection of statements from the Bible about the spirit, first in the Old Testament: 'In the beginning... the spirit of God swept over the face of the waters.' *(Genesis 1:1–2)*

In an older creation story, 'Then the Lord God formed man of dust from the ground, and breathed into his nostrils the breath (spirit) of life, and man became a living being.' *(Genesis 2:7)*

When the Israelites are on their way through the desert from Egypt, they are to build a tent in which to worship God. One man, Bezalel, is 'filled with a divine spirit, with skill, intelligence, and knowledge in every kind of craft.' *(Exodus 35:30–35)*

Later, the Spirit of God comes on Balaam and he utters oracles. *(Numbers 24:2–5)*

In 1 Samuel 10:10–13, Saul comes across a band of prophets, the Spirit of God comes on him and he prophecies.

Psalm 104:29–30 says to God, 'When you take away the breath of the animals they die and return to their dust. When you send forth your Spirit, they are created; and you renew the face of the ground.'

The prophet Isaiah declares, 'The Spirit of the Lord God is upon me, because the Lord has anointed me; he has sent me to bring good news to the oppressed...' *(Isaiah 61:1)*

The prophet Ezekiel is 'lifted up' by the Spirit, taken away and given visions of God's glory and judgement. *(Ezekiel 3:12 etc)*

Joel says there shall be a time of blessing and God will pour out his Spirit on all humanity: men, women, young and old. *(Joel 2:26–39)*

In the New Testament, Joseph is told that Mary's pregnancy is by the Holy Spirit. *(Matthew 1:20)*

Later, John the Baptist says that the coming Messiah will baptize with the Holy Spirit and with fire. *(Matthew 3:11)*

On one occasion, when criticized by the Pharisees, Jesus said, 'If it is by the Spirit of God that I cast out demons, then the kingdom of God has come to you.' *(Matthew 12:28)* In Luke 11:20 it is by 'the finger of God' that Jesus casts out demons.

In Luke's Gospel, the angel Gabriel tells Mary, 'The Holy Spirit will come upon you ... therefore the child to be born will be holy.' *(Luke 1:35)*

Then, when Jesus is baptized the Holy Spirit descends on him in bodily form, like a dove, and a voice comes from heaven, 'You are my Son, the Beloved; with you I am well pleased.' *(Luke 3:22)*

In John the risen Christ breathes on the disciples and says to them, 'Receive the Holy Spirit ...' *(John 20:22)*

In Acts, the sequel to Luke's Gospel, on the day of Pentecost the Holy Spirit comes on the disciples with a sound like a great wind and with tongues of fire, and they are able to speak with other languages, and with courage. *(Acts 2:1–4)*

Saint Paul writes on numerous occasions about the Spirit, for instance in Romans 8:2–27:

> *'The law of the Spirit of life in Jesus Christ has set you free from the law of sin and death...*
>
> *'All who are led by the Spirit of God are children of God...*
>
> *'When we cry 'Abba! Father!' it is that very Spirit bearing witness with our spirit that we are children of God...*
>
> *'The creation itself will be set free from its bondage to decay and will obtain the freedom of the glory of the children of God....*
>
> *'Likewise the Spirit helps us in our weakness; for we do not know how to pray as we ought, but that very Spirit intercedes with sighs too deep for words.'*

The Spirit gives various gifts to different people for the good of all: wise speech, knowledge, faith, gifts of healing, the working of miracles, prophecy, the ability to distinguish between spirits, tongues (or languages) and the interpretation of tongues. In this way the Church may be like a body, with different members valuing each other and working together.

The Spirit produces fruit: love, joy, peace, patience, kindness, generosity, faithfulness, gentleness, and self-control. *(Galatians 5:22)*

From this whole array of statements, which are only a few of the many that are in the Old and New Testaments, the Spirit is both continuously active, and works in specific ways and circumstances: the Spirit is both distant and close to the creation, and to humanity; the Spirit both works in the individual and develops community; the gifts, creations and activities of the Spirit are both strange, and very ordinary. As God is seen as both before or beyond, and working within the world, so too is the Spirit. The Spirit is the life and the life-giving facility of God.

Tuning in with the Spirit

For anyone who has a poor sense of pitch, but is keen to play the guitar, there is a simple technique for tuning the strings. Put a very small piece of paper on the string to be tuned, play the correct note on another string and slowly adjust the tuning key. When the string is in tune the piece of paper is thrown off the string by the vibration. When the string is at the right tension it vibrates, or resonates, in tune with the given note.

Some Christians would say that their praying is something like that; they are praying so that they can resonate with the life of the Spirit. Or, to return to the symbol of the wind, they are like a sailor who is trimming the sails in order to catch the optimum amount of wind. Unfortunately, to put it in terms of 'praying' is not necessarily helpful, as to many people the word 'praying' conjures up the activity of addressing words to God, either words they have learnt, read in a book, or are making up. These are ways of praying but there are many other ways as well. The difficulty is that the word 'prayer' can come to have such a fixed and narrow meaning that it is hard to think about other activities as the same kind of thing.

Some people prefer to talk about 'spirituality' as that can point to many other activities: meditation, singing, playing a musical instrument, dancing, painting, and so on. It might also suggest activities like going on a pilgrimage to a special place, or sitting quietly turning over concerns in one's mind with a sense of God in the situations, or scrubbing down a church hall to make it a temporary night shelter. The problem with the word 'spirituality' is that, unless one is aware that when one is talking about the Spirit one is talking about the dynamism of life itself, it can sound very vague and otherworldly. Neither term, 'prayer' or 'spirituality', is without its problems.

Even within the Christian Church there are a multitude of different ways in which people pray. Some are well established practices, others are things that have at times been thought suspect by the establishment but then been 'rediscovered'. Some are done individually, others in groups. It is also the case that many Christians do things which they feel and think help them become more themselves, more integrated, more able to cope and deal with difficult situations or more imaginative or relaxed, which they would not think of as prayer, or their spirituality. Bearing in mind the breadth of the activity of the Spirit within the minds of the writers of the Bible, this would be because their tradition has narrowed things down.

There has at times been a narrowing down of the understanding of the Spirit within the Church. Some of this has come from fear, and sometimes a well founded fear, when people have followed what they believed was the leading of the Spirit but it actually led to their own or other people's destruction or damage. Destructive cults are not a new phenomenon. Fear has led on occasion to an idea that only authorized officials of the Church were able to pass on the Spirit from person to person, and therefore the hierarchy could maintain control over the Church. Fear has also led to a denigration of the human body, as part of the rejection of the physical world as an ultimately worthless mess, which has meant that widely practised physical activities like dance, drama and the visual arts have sometimes not been seen as valid means of prayer. This denigration of the body and a fear of ecstasy has also led in some parts of the Church to sex being seen simply as a means of procreation, rather than also as a means of bonding, and recreation, in which the Spirit also has a part.

There has been change within this century. In many churches the leaders keep a fairly tight reign on what goes on within the congregations, through their rules and their ministers, but in the total life of the Church today a whole variety of practices go on. All sorts of things are now recognized by people within the Christian movement as being ways in which they can tune in with the Spirit, and develop what they need in order to become more integrated themselves, to build up community with others, and to live a life more in line with the ways of the Creator God. Some Christians pray using mantras and repetitive chants, others imagine their way into episodes in the Bible, others speak in tongues or lie on the floor, others dance or play the piano, some carve wood or arrange flowers, others cultivate gardens or paint.

As there now seems to be something of a rediscovery of the way of Jesus not as conformity with the systems of domination and exploitation of the world but as a way of creative challenge and reconstruction, so too there seems to be a rediscovery that life itself is the creation of the Spirit of God, and in the body, mind and imagination one can tune in to the music of the Spirit.

Prayer and Play

The similarities between prayer and play are quite striking. Like play, prayer often takes place when there is a sense of security. This sense may come from other people, who assure the person that it is all right to pray. More fundamentally it comes from a sense that God is to be trusted.

Someone moves off into an imaginative reading of a gospel passage or, perhaps with a phrase from one of the psalms in their mind, they begin to dance and transform the words into movement. They may simply feel that this is fun, and that the place and time are suitable for what they are doing; or, they may be a little more reflective, particularly if they are not used to doing this sort of thing. They may then be consciously trusting that this is all right, or even a good thing to do. They may even think it possible that in doing this they will attain a new sense of the ways of God, or somehow be a little more together as a result. If they thought it was a stupid thing to do, or believed that God was going to punish them for doing it, or that somehow they would come out of it damaged, they would not do it.

People also have different preferences in the ways in which they pray, as they do with playing. To some extent these match their personalities, and counterbalance the other activities that dominate their lives. It is also the case that some people are inhibited from praying in a certain way, even though it does in some ways appeal to them, because they fear it to be wrong. Even though they think it through and conclude otherwise, they feel that God does not really approve.

If they reflect on this further they might find that the God who does not approve has the face or voice of their father or mother and, once they have realized that, they might decide for themself whether or not to do it. For some people this may apply about praying in any way at all. As in the gospels, faith often involves actually striking out and doing something against inherited fears and taboos.

There are, of course, many situations when people pray which feel far from secure: the plane approaching an airport through a thunderstorm; the desperate illness of a child; the sound of approaching tanks. In these situations a person might call out to God for help, strength, healing, or safety. They might say a mantra or rosary, using this activity as a way of stilling or focusing their mind. They might imagine themself in the company of others — saints, martyrs, angels, or Jesus.

A number of things could be going on in this kind of situation. The person could have a fundamental sense that God is to be trusted, or is at least on their side, and so in the time of grave anxiety directs their concern towards God: 'God, you have helped us in the past; help us now.' The person using a type of prayer they are familiar with, is using it to tune in with God, and probably choosing a way which they have found helpful in the past. The security is not only in the attitude, but also in the familiarity of the activity. The most desperate prayer in this kind of situation is perhaps that of the person who cries out, 'God have mercy!' There they perhaps feel God to be at work in the threat. If they say these kind of words, presumably they assume there must be some chance that the threatening God will be merciful.

These kinds of prayer could hardly be described as playful. The urgency and terror of the situation remove anything that could be joyous. However, they do have the character of childlike behaviour. The child calls on the parent for help, for protection, or perhaps for relief from pain. An adult praying this way could be described as regressing to a childlike state. The person addresses the Creator as a parent. Though often a joyless prayer, it still has this imaginative characteristic.

Saint Paul on one occasion instructs his readers to pray at all times. He could hardly mean that people should spend every hour of every day meditating, speaking to God or praying in any kind of deliberate sense. The person who did so would be as tedious and anti-social as the person who could never be serious and get on with a job.

The Puritan, Jacob Astley, once prayed, 'Lord, you know how busy I must be today. If I forget you, do not forget me.' In the same way that sometimes even a child has to stop playing and get on with something, the same must apply with prayer. There are tasks to be done which need all our attention and concentrated effort. There are other things which are enjoyable in themselves, and could be spoiled by a person insisting on making them opportunities for prayer. The aunt who gives a jumper to her nephew hopes that the nephew will get on and wear it, not just keep writing polite letters of gratitude.

It is possible, however, for a person who in a piece of work is capable of serious and concerted effort and focused attention, to still be a playful person. This reflects their whole attitude to life, their ability to let go and enjoy things, to see the humour in a situation, and to live in the present rather than the past or the future. The same could be said of a prayerful person, and so perhaps they amount to the same thing. Like playing, prayer is an activity which takes up some periods of time, but not all. However the basic approach to life which enables play or prayer to happen, affects every activity.

Play invariably involves variety and has a balancing effect in a person's life. Even a person whose preferred play activity is doing crosswords is not going to do the same crossword over and over again. Play also invariably involves a degree of creativity, even if it is just doing an old thing in a new way.

Prayer is also a creative activity. In some ways of praying this is obvious, in others less so. There is a way of praying which involves saying the same phrase over and over again. The Jesus Prayer, widely used in the Orthodox Church is an example: 'Jesus, Son of God, have mercy upon me.' But even this repeated petition has a creative aspect as it becomes, in the person's mind, a kind of table over which other things can be spread, or a framework from which other thoughts and requests can arise. There are people who like to go to a church service where the same words are used every week, and they sometimes feel disappointed if they are changed. This is partly because the repetition of what are usually old words gives them a sense of continuity with their own past, and with the history of the Church. It is also sometimes the case that this familiar form of words is something out of which their own thoughts and meditations can arise. The creativity is not in the form of words but in their own reflections.

Most people probably feel that it is important to think about what we do. We might say this because we are aware that thinking is a capacity we have and which we should use if we are to lead balanced lives. This notion is likely to be reinforced by the common experience of making a mess of something and realizing afterwards that it was because we did not think about what we were doing. Many things make us think — television programmes, what other people say, bad feelings, needing to make decisions. In a church service the sermon is meant to help people to think. It may not succeed, but it will be clear to anyone in the church that it is a different thing from the prayers in the service. Similarly the prayers that are said may not help people to pray, but to most people present it will be clear that the sermon and the prayers are different kinds of activities.

This is because thinking and praying are not the same thing. Thinking is rather like work: it may be enjoyable and creative or it may be tedious and boring. But it is a focused activity with some kind of end product. Prayer is more like play. Play, be it in a sport, a hobby, or daydreaming on a bus, is a free activity, whose primary purpose is the enjoyment. Similarly the primary purpose of prayer is not sorting out ideas and drawing conclusions, it is the state of being there, in the Spirit.

Imagination is also an important feature of a lot of play, and of many types of prayer. Children imagine themselves to be in different situations when they play, and adults reading books or watching films enter into the story in what is often called 'suspended disbelief'. For the sake of the game they move in their imagination into another frame. This can happen in some kinds of prayer. A person may imagine they are in a scene in one of the gospels; they are there in their mind, hearing the sounds, smelling the dust and the bodies, and listening to what is being said. They might engage in discussion with one of the characters, or be one of the people taking part in the episode. They are engaging their imagination with the story and, in so doing, may realize something about their own life and situation.

Imagination has a much simpler function when a person addresses words to God. They are likely to call into their mind some image of God whom they are addressing. We have already considered the image of God as a parent figure who can help in a crisis. But a person may instead imagine Jesus standing there beside them. Jesus is obviously not there literally, in the same way that another person might be there in the room, but it is like someone writing a letter and having in their mind a picture of their friend to whom they are writing. They are addressing the words to that person, and so imagine them there as they form the words. Other images may come to mind — a light, flowing water, or the wind. Or God may be addressed as a parent, in the sense of one who values, cares about and hurts with their child, or provides correction and instruction to one who needs it.

Praying Together

We said of play that there was no proper way to do it; there might still be ways of playing which are good, and others which are not. While playing with other people, one needs to be aware of them. Young children at a toddler group will at first play separately in the same place and then slowly learn to play together. For older people rules can help a game take place without having to keep interrupting it to make decisions. The same is true of prayer; there is no proper way to do it; there may be good ways and bad ways. Many books are written to help people sort out ways of praying which are good for them, and how they can develop their spirituality.

From the beginnings of the Christian movement Christians have tended to pray both individually and together. The first Christians, being Jews, adapted the practices they were already familiar with and as time went on others developed. The temple declined in significance, and then disappeared completely. The synagogue and the private house became the main places for Christian corporate worship. Amongst Gentiles, the worship of Christian communities still owed a great deal to the practice of the synagogue, with its spoken prayers, readings from scripture and its sermon.

In the same way that people playing together need to have some kind of structure to help this happen, so too do people praying together. Whether people are playing a game or music, once there comes to be more than a few of them involved for anything more than a short period of time, some kind of organized framework is needed for the activity. This will generally involve either agreed rules, or leadership, or a combination of both. A small blues or jazz band can play together, developing a theme and passing the initiative from one to another. The separate minds and skills become almost one mind for a while, as the band becomes something more than the individual performers. But this will not always happen, and even a small band will find itself agreeing on some kind of structure before a performance, while a big band will also need to know quite clearly who is in charge.

The same applies when people come to pray together. Christian churches tend to have both rules and leaders. In some the emphasis may be on the rulebook, in others it may be on the worship leader. The purpose of the leadership and the rules is to help the congregation pray together in ways that are helpful to the participants.

However, it has to be acknowledged that it does not always work out that way. Insecurity can keep people enslaved to a rulebook instead of using it as a resource. Individuals can let their enjoyment of authority lead them to using their position of leadership for their own satisfaction rather than the good of the congregation which they are meant to lead. Leaders can come to use their position of authority or their skills and abilities to develop their own power within the group, and de-skill, or even oppress or abuse others. These are all problems in any organization. In churches there is an added significance and weight in that here people are dealing with what can be powerful symbols, and with something which is said to be not only a particular programme or cause, but about life itself.

When we look at the gospels we find that praying is not mentioned very much really. Jesus teaches his disciples not to pray by piling up words, as if God is more likely to hear them if they say a lot. Neither are they to make a show of what they are doing; they are to pray in 'a secret place', perhaps in the mind or in a private space. He also gave them a short form of words, now known as the Lord's Prayer, which could be something they would say together, as their community prayer, or as a hanger for other thoughts and prayers. *(Matthew 6:5–13 and Luke 11:1–4)* He taught them not to give up praying. *(Luke 11:5-10; 18:1-8)*

Jesus also spoke of a Pharisee and a tax collector going to a synagogue to pray. It was the tax collector, whose prayer was simply a recognition of himself as a sinner and a request for mercy from God, who was put into a positive relationship with God, rather than the Pharisee who expressed gratitude to God that he was much better than other people. *(Luke 18:9-14)*

Further to this there is an interesting episode in Matthew 21 when Jesus arrives in Jerusalem. We are told that the children ran around the temple shouting, 'Hosanna to the Son of David' and the priests wanted Jesus to make them be quiet. He refused, quoting a psalm which said that out of the mouths of young children God has brought perfect praise. It is impossible to know whether these children were playing or praying but Jesus was happy with it either way.

The priests in this story would have been more concerned about the words the children were using. Jesus was being referred to as the Son of David: the Messiah. Although it was not what Jesus called himself, he did not refuse the title. He clearly saw the rule of God coming about through what he was doing; there in the temple he was healing the blind and the lame. The first David had despised the blind and the lame, who were said to be forbidden entry to the first temple, but the worship of God was to be something to which all people were to have access.

Power, Reverence and Variety

Jesus also had strong words to say about power and authority. He said to his disciples:

> *'You know that among the Gentiles those whom
> they recognize as their rulers lord it over them, and
> their great ones are tyrants over them. But it is not so
> among you; but whoever wishes to be great among
> you must be your servant.'*

> *(Mark 10:42-43)*

It is ironic that in the seventeenth-century translation of the Bible the word used for servant was 'minister', as in church minister and prime minister. That is what the word 'minister' originally meant although there have been many in the Church and in politics who have seen the role as an opportunity for domination.

In Matthew's Gospel Jesus says:

> *'You are not to be called teacher (rabbi), for you*
> *have one teacher and you are all students. And call*
> *no-one your father on earth, for you have one*
> *Father, the one in heaven. Nor are you to be called*
> *instructors, for you have one instructor, the Messiah.*
> *The greatest among you will be your servant.'*
>
> (Matthew 23:8–11)

It is sometimes said that prayers need to be appropriate to God, and to the occasion: one cannot just make up prayers, or simply do what one feels like or wants to do. It is God the Creator to whom one prays, not some benign uncle or schoolfriend. Prayer, it might be said, should be characterized by reverence, respect, and decorum.

One needs to ask for whose benefit this attitude of reverence is adopted. Jesus taught his disciples to address God as *Abba*, their father, using the familiar term that a person might use towards their own parent. He also warned against piling up 'empty phrases' in prayer, as if God was more likely to listen to a lot of long words than a few short ones. He endorsed the attitude of the Old Testament Psalmist who said of God, 'Out of the mouths of babies and infants you have brought perfect praise.' Following this line God is not going to be outraged or offended at the informality and presumption of a person who prays by talking to God as if God was a friend of the family.

However, it might be good for the person praying to also use other ways of praying which open their mind and feelings to God being more than a family friend, to being the ground of all existence, and ultimately a mystery. This may be assisted by an atmosphere or attitude of what is commonly called reverence. But it may not; it may be better assisted by the person practising a form of meditation or art. People differ and what helps one person may not help another; exploration is necessary.

Different Christian traditions have developed different ways of trying to draw the minds or emotions of congregations into a sense of wonder and awe of God. While medieval Catholics had developed elaborate rituals, many Protestants in reaction reduced their ceremonies to the bare minimum and their buildings to a stark simplicity. While the one tried to capture the sense of the glory of God in complexity, the other took the line that this could not be captured, nor attempted, and therefore took a minimalist approach to ritual and decoration. It is possible to see both approaches as having something to commend them, and for spiritual explorers to draw from a variety of traditions.

It is also notable that different traditions have drawn ideas and practices from each other in recent decades. Catholics will meet for silence or for free prayer, whilst Presbyterians will be found lighting candles and singing chants.

A number of things have enabled this kind of development. One has been a change of mind on the part of many who lead corporate worship so that they do not ask, 'What is the right thing to do?' but, 'What will help the people worship?' Another is a willingness on the part of at least some leaders to relinquish power in their congregations and to let other people be involved in the preparation, planning and leading of services. Whilst demands for an attitude of reverence and order in worship have something to commend them, they also mean that the leaders remain very much in charge of what is happening, and this authority can be abused. Other people can become dependent on them in an unhealthy way, or unable to develop the rich potential of their own spirituality.

Play, Worship and the Healing Cycle

Looking back again at the healing cycle which we considered in chapter five we can perhaps see prayer and play both as important ways of engaging in that process. A person may pray initially through pleasure, or discipline. In other words a prayer may be a spontaneous response that comes from wonder — the sort of praising God that the writers of the psalms capture — arising from awe at the sky or the significance of humanity. On the other hand a person may pray because that is what they have planned to do at that particular time. But, as we considered in chapter five, prayer can also arise from grief, struggle or sadness. Psalm 130 begins, 'Out of the depths I cry to you, O Lord'.

When this happens the person is coming to God, whom they see as a Nurturing Parent, in the Sad Child mode. On some occasions perhaps they see God as the Critical Parent, and apologize for the wrong they have done. But in this particular situation they see God as caring and compassionate, and they trust in God's welcome, and God's being with them.

This activity, which is prayer, is also in some senses play. The person praying believes it to be true that God is caring and compassionate, that God does not hold against a person their failures and the wrongs they have done, and God does not ignore their pain but is involved in it with them. In their imagination, they have God located in that place with them. God, they believe, is specifically there. They may address God in words or they might remain silent, like a child held by a parent. They receive the energy which they need to go out again: free and creative.

This focusing of the mind may be assisted by a drama. The most commonly acted out drama in the Church is of the Last Supper that Jesus had with his disciples before his crucifixion. Time and again in the gospels Jesus ate meals with people, and he was criticized for the table company he kept. In the Holy Communion service the story of this last supper is told, and with bread and wine it is partly re-enacted.

During that service a person may imagine being in that gathering before Jesus' crucifixion, or at a meal with Jesus and a crowd of tax collectors, or with the disciples who meet with Jesus and share bread after his rising again. There is a continuity here in what is being said and done; they can see themselves as part of the same thing. In taking part in that drama, people are sometimes particularly helped in having a sense of God welcoming them, forgiving them, holding them, and then letting them go out into the future that is just beginning, in the power of the Spirit. It is a game, a kind of play, as is a great deal of prayer. But it is a way in which many people are enabled to see life in a different way, and get on with living with energy and freedom. They are convinced that it is a means by which God the Creator restores them to a more complete life and gives them the strength they need to recognize God's rule in the world and to work to realize it.

The word 'worship' is often used when people are talking about prayer. It comes from an older English word, 'worthship', meaning to give someone what was due to them. If the god being worshipped is conceived of as unpredictable, unfriendly or demanding then trying to give it what is its due could lead to all sorts of destructive rituals. But the worship of the creative God, as taught and portrayed by Jesus, would involve practices which work for the healing of broken people, and their tuning-in with God's life. God's concern is the good of creation, not the satisfying of some craving for honour and acclamation.

When we considered the healing cycle earlier we also noted how the three movements — the welcome, the workout and the departure — would be characteristics of any effective therapy and of the prayer of an individual, if that person is going to be strengthened or enabled to live more wholly and fully. They will also be characteristics of a person's participation in a group's worship of God, if that is going to help the person.

In the worship of a group of people, the welcome will involve a person being helped to grasp the fact that they are welcomed by God and are not unsuccessfully banging at the doors of heaven. It is, of course, hard to see how a person can have that sense of welcome if they do not feel welcomed by the other people taking part in the worship.

The workout can take place in a number of ways. It might be a very cerebral activity, through the meaning of the words in the prayers, bible readings or sermon or it might be more in the music, the colour, the movement, the ritual and the visual symbols. These things may simply be a pleasant performance. However, they can be things which help a person work through their dilemmas or difficulties, or open up new avenues of creativity and possibility, through the use of the right brain, or even tapping into the unconscious through archetypal symbols.

The group activity must lead on to the people being able to go out from the meeting or service, probably on their separate ways. This is not only a practical necessity, that the caretaker wants to lock up or they need to have something to eat or drink, but follows from the sense of God as Creator. In the multitude of other activities of each person's life they are also involved with God. God is as interested in these activities as in the religion. Some of the prophets believed that God was more interested in social justice and community than in religious worship; there are no churches mentioned in the first chapter of Genesis. Bishop John Taylor, the author of *The Go-Between God*, said that God is more interested in people being alive than in their being religious.

The Need for Change

Religious practice exists to help people tune in to what God is about and become more fully alive. In as much as it fails to do this there is something wrong with it. That does not necessarily mean it needs abolishing, although some people who have had an overdose of bad religion may be better off avoiding it for a while. What it does mean is that if it fails it needs changing.

What needs to be changed may be with regard to any one of the three phases of the cycle of healing. The church may be unwelcoming or it might welcome newcomers and visitors with great warmth, but generate an idea that they are not really welcomed by God, at least not until they have performed particular rituals, had particular experiences, made an acceptable act of commitment, or learnt how to talk with the right kind of jargon.

The church might also fail to let people go, keeping them in a state of childish dependency on the leader or the institution, in fear of their own ability to question and think, or of the world outside the fold of faith. It might also fail to help people in the crucial central phase of the workout. One way of attending to this is to give people the personal attention they need to talk through the things in their lives that cause them to be less than they might be. If the leader of a church expects to be able to do this with all the members of his or her congregation they will only achieve it by having a very small church. Small groups where people can get to know each other and develop trust and friendships clearly assist in this process, as people help each other. Those with particular skills and experience then only need to be called in from the group to provide the help they can give, as and when necessary. But even then these may not be the leaders of the church, but simply other members of a wider group who have something they can offer which can help in this particular situation.

The other way that this phase can be assisted is by encouraging or helping people to pray imaginatively and playfully, both as individuals and together. This is not to exhort people to pray more, or to come more often to church services, but to help people develop their ways of praying, in the broadest sense of the word, and integrate that into their lives, so that people are encouraged to sing, paint, dance, go for walks, write poems and plays, meditate, carve wood, grow trees, visit particular places, tell stories and, in other words, do any of the multitude of things that might enrich their lives and help them be more together and whole. And to do this individually and together.

If this happens prayer and worship can increasingly become activities which engage the depths of the person and the group, and draw together diffused and different aspects of the self. Much of the necessary work within a person, for them to become more whole, will then happen not through a deliberate and structured therapy but unconsciously and quietly — the Spirit moving in the depths of the individual as well as in the interaction between people. If prayer is seen as a kind of play this might help people approach it in a way which is more open to its creative possibilities than if it is considered as a kind of dutiful work.

1   Based on a story from *Rolling in The Aisles* © Murray Watts 1987. Used by permission of Kingsway Publications, Eastbourne.

CHAPTER EIGHT
LIVING FAITH

OVERVIEW

The Double Focus

The hunting owl has a depth of vision because its two eyes enable it to see from two different positions. We humans have the same ability. As our minds receive images from our two eyes they appreciate the solidity of objects and also judge distance and direction. With the engineering of sound in a stereophonic music system a sense of depth is created with sounds from two different sources. In this book we have been bringing together images from two different ways of thinking about the world, looking at some key images that we use in understanding the world and relating those to key images in the Bible.

We thought about what the writings in the Bible were, in relation to the different kinds of learning that people are involved in, and I suggested that the Bible should be thought of as a possible source of wisdom, rather than knowledge in the scientific sense. Turning then to the way that we think about the world in our own time, we saw that, whilst the Bible came from societies with a very different way of understanding the world, some of the biblical writings could add to our own appreciation and evaluation of the universe we are part of.

Then we looked at the work and the teaching of Jesus. We looked at his healing activity in the light of a psychological understanding of the ways that people interact. We then took this further to think about the phenomenon of human violence and what Jesus taught about dealing with violence. In this area the teaching and actions of Jesus provide a key image for thinking about how we live together which contrasts with many of the assumptions and practices of our society and provides an alternative to destructive violence.

Finally we considered the almost universal activity of play and I suggested that praying could be seen in many respects as a kind of playing. In this case the experiences of wonder and play provide a framework for thinking about the practice of prayer which enables it to be seen as a feature of life rather than an otherworldly activity. Prayer can then perhaps be seen as a skill or ability which any person can develop from their innate abilities.

In doing all this we have been making a mental step over two thousand or more years of intellectual history. The way people saw the world in the Eastern Mediterranean at the time of Jesus and before, and the way that people in Western society see things now are very different. But I believe we have been able to bring together insights from these very different periods and cultures in a way that provides a depth of vision. It will be worth thinking for a moment about how this has happened, because it has not been straightforward.

The ways that the different key images have come together has varied according to what it is we have been thinking about. In considering the nature of the universe — space and ecosystems — we were looking at the subject from different angles and the biblical wisdom complemented the scientific understanding. When thinking about the healing activity of Jesus, the psychological understanding enabled us to see the practice of Jesus in a way that made it applicable to a variety of other situations. When developing this to think about Jesus' response to violence his attitude and teaching appeared in sharp contrast with what has been generally considered normal behaviour in Western society for many centuries.

However, in doing this we were not treating the words and action of Jesus as a timeless vision but understanding them using the assumptions and practices of current Western historical research. Our picture of Jesus emerged as a result of our treating the gospel narratives and the person of Jesus as belonging in a particular culture. His talk about 'turning the other cheek' and 'going an extra mile' were seen as relating to particular situations which would have arisen in Jesus' society, but which provide images of a way of dealing with things which can arise in any society. Here, the current Western perspective made clear the significance of what is embedded in the gospels.

Finally, we reflected on the phenomena of wonder and play in a way that is characteristic of Western thinking. This then provided a setting for understanding traditional practices of prayer and worship which suggested ways that these practices might be developed.

There has not been one simple way in which one perspective has fitted with another, but holding the two views together has involved moving back and forth. This has perhaps had something of the untidiness of a conversation or a dialogue. Or, to put it in visual imagery, it has possibly been like putting together a set of photographs of a building taken from different places and angles.

In the same way the processes of seeing in depth or listening to music are not neat and straightforward. With two eyes we perceive the same image from slightly different angles and this enables the depth of view, but actually looking at something to see what it is like involves a random scanning, moving our eyes from one point to another. And whilst our ears continuously receive sounds the process of listening involves moving our attention from one or two sounds to others and then back again, in a similar kind of way. In this book we have been trying to listen to what different sources say, or to see things in depth by looking from different angles.

Relating the two views might have been neater if we had simply seen one view in terms of the other. If we had tried to interpret the Christian tradition in the light of modern understanding, or subjected the current Western way of viewing the world to criticism from the perspective of traditional Christian teaching, the process might have been more straightforward. And both these kinds of thinking go on within the Church.

However, there are serious problems with these approaches. We saw in the opening chapters how people's ways of understanding the world shift over time and took the paradigm shifts inaugurated by Copernicus and Newton as examples of the kind of process that takes place. There have been hundreds of other movements and changes over the years such that the Western way of seeing the world in the present time is quite different from that of Jesus' time and culture. We also now have an awareness that there are such differences and that changes are continually taking place. What is currently a widely accepted way of thinking about the world could itself change in time.

We can also be aware of limitations and weaknesses within our own cultural outlook. The ecological crisis and the way that Western society at present seems impotent in dealing with violence are just two problems that many people are aware of. So to suggest that Christianity simply be reinterpreted to fit in with Western cultural assumptions and attitudes is to ignore the weaknesses and limitations of this culture. At the same time, to take a stand on something described as 'Christian teaching', be it authorized by a particular church leadership or a particular traditional way of interpreting the Bible, is to ignore the way that every perspective is bound in a particular culture. There is not a body of timeless truths. There are simply the insights of people who all have their own assumptions and ways of seeing the world of which they are part.

Both these other approaches also ignore the fact that what is at the root of Christian faith is confidence in a person. In all their diversity the writings of the New Testament relate one way or another to the teaching, life, death and resurrection of Jesus, a man of a particular time and place. He was not totally beyond or outside his culture. When the first Christians came to write the gospels they did not present a set of disembodied ideas but wrote about him and they were all keen to say that he belonged in a particular place (Galilee and Judea) and in a particular period (the time of Pontius Pilate). The process of Christian learning is inevitably going to involve mentally stepping back and forth between the cultures of Jesus and the writers of the Bible, and our own.

Images of Jesus

The first followers of Jesus were engaged in a similar task to ourselves. The Christian movement spread out from Palestine in all directions among people of different cultures. Though they lived at the same time and the differences were not as pronounced as they are between the culture of the biblical writers and our own, they still had some interpreting to do and, in the process of doing that, their thinking developed. This development was not new; from the time when the first psalm or story was put down on papyrus, the thinking of the biblical writers altered and adjusted in different circumstances and with new insights. There was also difference of emphasis and interest among different people. The Bible does not come to us as a monolithic intellectual system; it arose from the struggles, experiences, visions and ideas of a multitude of people, and contains all the variations and inconsistencies one would expect of such a collection of documents. Nevertheless there was a common theme, which was to do with God, the world and people.

The first followers of Jesus had what they believed was good news about God, the world and people, and they were concerned to try to get that news across to others. As a result of their attempts, and their success, the movement grew rapidly. They wrote books and letters which came to be gathered together as the books of the New Testament, they produced a host of other writings, and the movement very slowly came to be organized as the Church.

It is worth remembering that there never was one organization called 'the Church'. There were always a number of associated, affiliated networks, meetings, groups and individuals. They called the groups 'churches'. They thought of all of these churches' members together as the whole Church. But they were never organized as one church. Sometimes they were not clear about who was part of the Church and who was not and sometimes they argued furiously about it. As time went on they became more organized, with affiliations looking to one central church or leader — Rome, Antioch or Alexandria — but they were never organized as one. Even in the feudal Middle Ages in Europe when leadership and power in the Church was vested very much in the Bishop of Rome, there was at least one other Church over in the East with its patriarchs, bishops and congregations; another one in Ethiopia, and one in India.

In all this change and diversity, the basic writings of the first Christians encouraged them to continue to look to Jesus for inspiration and guidance. It has to be recognised that the churches have not always been very good at that — sometimes it has been a very hard task. Thinking about how some of the churches have been at times, and some of the things they have done, it is hard to see how anyone believed that this had any connection with what Jesus of Nazareth was about, though no doubt they did. We will not go into details; it is easy enough to find a history book which will provide horror stories about the Church; sometimes a newspaper would do.

However, in the early Church the person of Jesus was central. The

Christian movement was about Jesus; the good news was centred on him. So a part of the intellectual activity of the first Christians was trying to make sense of who Jesus was, and what his possible significance was for other people.

Jesus' immediate followers dealt with him as a man. He was a teacher and a one time carpenter from the village of Nazareth in Galilee. They listened to what he said, watched what he did, shared meals and had conversations with him. They tried to do what he told them, but they made a lot of mistakes, and they let him down. They were involved with him, as any other disciples might be involved with their teacher.

Later, after his crucifixion, they were involved with him in a different way. As they talked about him with other people, and invited them to be involved with Jesus, they could not just introduce them to the man: 'Here is Jesus. Come along with him.' It was a different kind of involvement, and called for more explanation. The explanations about Jesus began from their own experience. As they thought about and talked about that, and as other people became involved, they developed a number of ways of describing Jesus. In doing this they used images that they drew from both their Jewish and their non-Jewish background, often using words and ideas which were part of the common thinking of the time. Their aim was to make a connection with other people's lives and experience as well as to make sense, for their own sake, of who Jesus was and what he was about.

The words and terms that they used then stayed in use, even though people's ways of thinking changed. This was inevitable as the first Christians were the founders and what they had said was the base from which others worked. The fact that their writings were collected and preserved meant that future generations could relate directly to them, and even several hundred years on, they could still be the second Christians. They did not have to be dependent on centuries of tradition and change if they chose to go back to the early writings.

But there was a problem; as time went on, although the writings might be accessible, the ideas were not necessarily as easy to grasp. The social context had changed and words came to have different meanings: a term which would have rung with a particular significance in the first century might have very different associations in another era and society. So it is that today in the Church there is an array of different words which are used about Jesus which were once everyday terms but are now only used in a religious setting. They are used in prayers and hymns, and of course found in the Bible, but are not words which have an immediate meaning for people in the way that they did when first used centuries ago. And if they do have a meaning it might be different from when it was first used to talk about Jesus. Therefore it is worth considering some of these words, and thinking what they meant to the first Christians.

• *The Messiah*

We have thought about this title already in chapter six. Through what Jesus was doing the Rule, or kingdom, of God was coming about. 'Messiah' was an old term, going right back to the first kings of ancient Israel. A messiah was literally someone 'anointed by Yahweh'. The ceremony of kingmaking involved pouring oil or ointment onto the person's head. Someone anointed by Yahweh was not just any king, he was Yahweh God's king.

In time of exile and occupation the later Jews came to look forward to the coming of a new Messiah. A number of people claimed the title. The first Christians reckoned that it belonged to Jesus. Most of the first Christians spoke Greek and it was in Greek that they wrote their books and letters. The Greek word that had been used earlier as a translation of Messiah was *Christos*. Jesus was the *Christos*. It became almost a second name, and they, his people, became the 'Christians'.

• *The Son of Man*

The Son of Man seems to have been the title that Jesus of Nazareth used for himself. At its most basic it simply means a man. The prophet Ezekiel had been addressed in his visions as 'Son of man', by another being that was not a human being but some kind of angelic figure. Then in one of the strange fantasies of the apocalyptic book of Daniel, a figure appears who is described as 'like a son of man', in contrast to all the angelic beings and beasts who have appeared so far. This son of man is given power over all the peoples of the world. He becomes a universal king.

To following generations of Jews, including those of Jesus' own time, the term 'son of man' would have had a messianic ring to it. A son of man was a human being but the Son of Man was also the Messiah. As the Messiah, the Son of Man might have been seen as a Jewish king, but he might also have been seen as a representative figure for all humanity, so that the Son of Man was seen as a universal person. The title dropped out of common use amongst Christians. Though Saint Paul thought about Jesus as a universal person he did not use this term, possibly because it would have meant little to Greek-speaking Gentiles. In Western culture now it would also have little meaning.

The most notable thing about the phrase to many people would be its double masculinity. In an English-speaking world that is struggling to adapt its language to develop terms which include both male and female people without bias, it is a title which might be considered more unhelpful than meaningless although in its Old Testament origin it was used to differentiate a human being from an angelic being or spiritual power, rather than to make any point about the masculinity of the prophet or the Messiah. This is why the translators of the New Revised Standard Version of the Bible use the term 'mortal' in Ezekiel, and 'human being' in Daniel, though they keep the phrase 'Son of Man' in the gospels.

• The Lord

The Greek word, *Kyrios*, could be applied to anyone, from a respected teacher to the Roman Emperor, and to God. When people in the gospels called Jesus 'Kyrios' they were not necessarily meaning anything more than respect. Disciples would call their teacher Kyrios. He was their leader — the one to be listened to, and to be taken seriously. They might argue with him, but in the end, if they were going to be consistent as disciples, the Lord was to be obeyed.

• Son of God

The Kyrios title took on another ring as well. In his prayers Jesus had addressed God directly as his father. The word he used was the word a child used of its parent: Abba. Jesus also taught his disciples to do the same. He gave them a new relationship with the Creator God.

To address the Creator as Abba could seem quite absurd. To those who were concerned to look after God's dignity for him it would seem blasphemous. But Jesus was insistent, about this and about its implications for his disciples:

> *You are not to be called rabbi for you have one*
> *teacher and you are all students. And call no-one*

> *your father on earth, for you have one Father — the*
> *one in heaven. Nor are you to be called instructors,*
> *for you have one instructor, the Messiah.*
>
> (Matthew 23:8-10)

If God was the father, they were God's children. But Jesus was the first: he was the Son. Paul put it in terms of Jesus being the son who was born that way while the others were God's adopted children. Stories at the beginning of Matthew's and Luke's Gospel tell of Jesus being born as God's Son by the power of the Holy Spirit.

• *The Word made flesh*

Paul also spoke of Jesus as being the image of the invisible God. At the beginning of his gospel John spoke of the *logos* or 'Word' of God. The *logos* for him, and many Greeks of the time, was the reason, the logic, or the meaning of things. People who looked for understanding were looking for *logos*. This Word was God, and with God at the beginning, and everything that was made was made by the Word. Then the Word was made a person, a human being, whom others could see, meet with and trust in; that person was Jesus. It was as if there was a light that shines for every person, and that light came into the world in Jesus.

Later generations of theologians took this idea of the Word 'becoming flesh' and talked about the 'Incarnation' of the Word, which is another way of saying the same thing. The whole event of God being involved in the world in Jesus came to be referred to as the Incarnation.

The first Christians did not think of themselves as telling people something about which they knew nothing. Much of it was there for them to see in the world around them and in the insights of prophets and poets. What they wanted people to know was that the understanding or purpose that they were looking for was there in Jesus and, through him, the possibility of a new way of relating to other people, to the world and to the Creator.

• *The Saviour*

One of the things that everyone was aware of was that the world was not how it might be. The world for all its beauty and wonder, which some could appreciate, and all its opportunities, which some could take, was something of a mess. A whole system was built on violence, fear and domination.

Looking at themselves honestly, most people would consider that they were not all they might be either. They might think themselves to be something of a mess. Sometimes the inadequacy or disease might be physical; sometimes it was within the mind. Sometimes it was a matter of trying to live with memories of past errors and mistakes.

But Jesus was not some celestial being, untouched by all the seething power struggles, jealousy, injustice and violence of human society. Jesus was a man who had been caught up in it all, to the extent of being tortured and executed by the government. Jesus knew what it was like to be caught up in the mess of human society. He also showed that God's attitude was one of creating and offering new opportunity, not of leaving people to struggle with their past failures. God had also brought Jesus through his death into a new kind of life, called 'resurrection', and God could be trusted to do the same for people who joined in with what Jesus was about.

The word they used for the mess the world was in and for individual moral wrongdoing was *hamartia*. It is usually translated 'sin'. What God does with individual sins is to send them away into the bin of history. He forgives, and the person has a new start in the present moment. God has overcome the sin of the world in the death of Jesus, when all the power of the old order, built on violence and domination, could not get the better of him. God is now, they say, in the process of re-ordering society. The new order — based on active concern and compassion, or 'love', is being established. Jesus is the Saviour, the one who rescues us from the old order of distortion, oppression and death, and brings us into the new order of his rule.

• *The Redeemer*

Put like that it could sound rather forbidding; moving from a mess to a new order might be constricting or confining. There is sometimes something rather welcoming about disorder. Order, in the sense of uniformity and regimented neatness could be oppressive. The new order that the first Christians spoke of was not another form of the imperialist order of Rome, but was characterized by freedom.

Their experience of moving into Jesus' movement, of knowing that their past sins were behind them and that the sin of the world did not have control of them was like being liberated from slavery. They were entering into a whole new world of freedom and hope. Jesus was therefore also the Redeemer, the one who sets slaves or prisoners free.

For redemption there was a price to be paid; Jesus had paid with his life. By his actions and his words, Jesus had declared God's forgiveness of sinners, his welcome of the reject and the coming of the new order of love. He had stuck to his declaration right through his trial to his death, and God had affirmed this in his resurrection.

• *The High Priest*

Jesus was also the Priest. Priests were a kind of go-between. People brought their gifts for the god to the priest, and the priest did what was needed to pass them on. The priest would represent the people to the god, and represent the god to the people. He belonged to both and stood between.

Following Jesus, priests were not needed any more as people could address the one God directly. They could pray themselves and they could learn directly from God, through the Spirit. They would help each other learn, and pray for each other. Some people might have special responsibilities within the community to pray for others or to help them realise the love of God.

But there were no go-betweens except that, on occasion, anyone might be a go-between for anyone else: praying for them, helping them see things about God, helping them know they were forgiven and free. There was one Priest: Jesus. He had stood between people and God, bringing knowledge of the love of God to people and bringing their human experience into the life of God. The Jewish temple practice with its priests and sacrifices was swept away in AD 70 when the temple was destroyed by the Romans. Other religions continued to have their priests, but not the Church.

In time the word 'priest' did come to be used of worship leaders in many parts of the Church, and some churches came to teach that these people were go-betweens appointed by God for the people. It is hard to find that idea in the New Testament, and it has been rejected by many churches, including ones who still keep the title for some of their ministers.

The Trinity

Christian thinking did not stop at using various images and arguments to get across to people the significance of Jesus, and what involvement with him was about. As time went on Christian teachers coined a new image to make sense of something else which was a part of their experience of God.

A person might have a sense of God beyond the world: God the artist Creator whose universe shows something of himself; God whose prophets speak of justice for the oppressed and compassion for the failure and the rejected; God whose agents have worked in history to liberate slaves, establish communities of mutual respect and support, and speak wisdom to the confused.

A person might also have a sense of God in Jesus. In the dealings of this man with others, in his teaching, in his healing of the sick and his declarations of forgiveness, in his standing before the Jewish Council and Pilate, and in his crucifixion, one was seeing God.

A person might also have a sense of God the Spirit at work, within the community, in the individual, within the creation: giving insight and courage, pleasure and hope, concern and peace; bringing out new gifts and skills in people; drawing together people of different backgrounds and cultures so they could trust and respect each other as brothers and sisters; creating life in all its dimensions.

The simple declaration of the Church's teachers was that these were all different senses or experiences of God. They were not three different powers, either at odds or in alliance with each other. They were simply God, known in three ways: God the Father, God the Son and God the Holy Spirit.

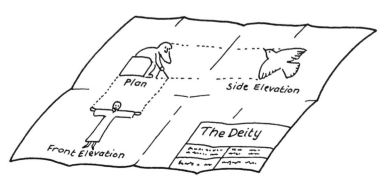

Someone at some point coined the word 'Trinity'. A unity is one thing; the Trinity is both three and one at the same time.

There are plenty of things which are experienced in three different ways. Music can be written in a book and seen as dots on lines, it can be heard being played as a sequence of sounds, and it can be entered into so that one is caught up in it. Lilac can be seen in a garden as a shrub with leaves and branches and roots, it can be seen in a decoration as a flower and it can be smelt as a perfume. They are all music or all lilac: one thing, or three.

Christian thinkers also wrestled with questions of how Jesus of Nazareth was related to God. People experienced God in Jesus, but what was going on in the mind of Jesus between him and God? How was the Spirit related to the Father? In the first few centuries they used the concepts available to them at the time, mainly drawing on branches of Greek philosophy.

Some of these came to be fossilized by parts of the Church as if they were truths for all time, though there has always eventually been someone who has decided that the issues had to be thought through again. In the same way that people like Copernicus and Galileo have produced new key ideas to make sense of the information available about the nature of the world, so too there have been theologians down the centuries who have worked to make sense of the human experience of God.

Rethinking has had to take place as new information, new technology and continual discoveries mean that people's understanding of the world they are part of changes as time goes on. The work of theology is to try to make sense of this with reference to the big questions about meaning and value, and the varieties of human experience. This century has not only seen atomic fission but also Hiroshima; not only the development of sophisticated organizational skills, but also Auschwitz; not only moon landings but also the slow death by starvation of millions. Theologians must not only concern themselves with ancient ideas but with new human experiences such as these, with the questions, challenges and insights that come from other religious traditions, and with future possibilities as human life causes irreversible change to the life systems of the planet.

The work of theology also continues because new information becomes available. Jesus and the first Christians belong there in history. They have not changed, but there is information now available as a result of historical and archaeological research which means that people are able to understand things about the social context of Jesus' life which were not understood by people working in Italy or Greece in the third or fourth century. Christian teaching is not fixed for all time, but the research, the thinking and the interpretation goes on although, in the end, it is not the ideas that matter.

Living Faith

Jesus never asked anyone whether they believed that he was the Son of God, the Messiah, or the second person of the Trinity. He once asked his disciples who they thought he was. He was called Rabbi, Lord, and Son of David, and he did not quibble. But he never checked whether people had the right ideas in their minds about who he was or what he was doing. He responded to their trust in him which was something that he commended in people. People heard about him, listened to him, watched what he did, and some of them trusted him. The ideas and the understanding came later, if they came at all.

A word that crops up time and again in English translations of the Bible and particularly in the New Testament, is the word 'faith'. It translates a Greek word *pistis*, but there is a crucial difference between the way the English and the Greek words are used. In English we talk about 'having faith', almost as if faith is something someone can possess. But in Greek it is not like that: there is a verb, *pisteo*, and so in Greek one does not have faith, one does it.

This means that it is possible to talk and think about faith now, in English, as if it were a set of ideas one might have in one's mind, or even a collection of rituals which have become a part of one's lifestyle. We might think of having faith like someone might have a good understanding of Freudian psychology, or a diet which is good for their teeth. In English people even talk sometimes about 'the Christian faith', as if it was a bundle of ideas and practices which someone might choose to adopt.

But the first Christians did not think like that and neither did Jesus himself. When Jesus commended the woman with the haemorrhage for her faith he was referring to the way in which she trusted that she could go out and touch him and that it would do her good, rather than bring about a punishment from God. And when he turned to Jairus, the ruler of the synagogue who was standing nearby, he said that he too needed to have this attitude. What Jesus said is usually translated into English as 'Have faith', or 'Believe', because in English we cannot talk about 'faithing' — our language does not permit it. But it could be put better as, 'Trust me'.

Jairus was faced with the news that his daughter had died. He was now caught in a swirl of grief, anxiety and uncertainty. Jesus said, 'Trust me'. In other words, 'Keep hold of your confidence in me for a bit longer, and we'll see where it goes' *(Mark 5:36)*. Trusting people is sometimes like that. People are always something of a mystery. Trusting someone sometimes means believing that they are concerned for your good, even when what they are up to is a puzzle. But it is this attitude of trust that Jesus commended, which is fundamentally a trust in God.

The people like the woman with the haemorrhage, Jairus and the friends of the man lowered down from the roof, trusted Jesus. But they were calling on him for something which they believed God could give them; they saw Jesus as the means or the channel for this so their trust was perhaps twofold. Basically they trusted that they mattered to God and that God would be concerned about their situation and their difficulty. They also trusted that God could respond to their appeal for help through this man, Jesus. But it is also possible that they had come to have the trusting attitude towards the Creator God because of what they had heard from, or about, Jesus.

Therefore now, if someone is going to be involved with Jesus, the basic requirement is trust. There is certainly a place for questioning and exploration, for finding out what other people's experiences are, for weighing things up and seeing if it makes sense, but what is needed is trust in God, rather than having every question answered and everything clear.

That might mean looking at the night sky and saying to oneself, 'It is beyond my comprehension but, whatever it is that is behind it all is good'.

It might mean saying to oneself when one has been sent from office to office and waited for letters that haven't come, and spoken to people on the phone who don't seem to know anything about you and don't seem to care, 'Hang on! I matter and I may not matter to you. I may not matter to anyone else, but I matter, in myself. I matter to God, and I deserve better than this.'

It might mean hearing of seals being washed up dying with metal poisoning and saying to oneself, 'This should not happen. They are only seals, and there are plenty of them, and we do not need them, but they matter. They matter to God.'

It might mean reading of Jesus dealing with a devious question from the authorities, standing his ground and replying with humour, and saying, 'Yes, that is it. That is what is needed. Not to fight back or to just let it happen, but to reply creatively, respecting their dignity as people, and claiming my own. And working out how to do that myself.'

It might mean praying, being quiet and still and saying, 'God, I want to join in with what you are about. Help me to do that and to know what to do.'

It might mean reminding oneself that the past is gone, the failure is forgiven, and the present is a new created moment.

It might mean going to a group of Christians and saying, 'I think Jesus got it right. I want to join in with what you are doing.'

It might mean saying to oneself, 'I cannot go along with all that. It might hurt but I have to move out into another space now. I have to leave and see where God takes me.'

Faith may mean a number of things, but fundamentally it means responding to God with trust. It is not assent to a set of propositions or holding a set of ideas, it is trust in God. We develop our ideas, learning both on our own and from other people, though all the time God remains beyond them.

That is true of the universe; however much we study it, it will always remain something of a mystery, but we get on with living in it. It is true of ourselves: we do not understand a lot of what is going on in our heads, but we still make our decisions. It is true of other people: we know them less than we know ourselves, but we still often trust them. So it must be with God.

Following On

In this book I have been attempting to make sense of some of the wisdom and insights of the Bible, and particularly of Jesus himself, within the way of thinking about the world which is widely held in Western society at this period in its history. What follows are two appendices: one appendix lists other books which may be helpful to anyone who wants to take some of this thinking and exploration further:

the other lists details of a few of the many organizations and groups which are working at ways of responding creatively to some of the challenges we face as a society.

Some of the organizations I have listed aim to develop their policies from a Christian base or to work out in a consciously Christian and creative way how they will respond to issues, but not all of them. The organizations are listed simply so that anyone who is moved to get involved with an organization which is addressing issues of ecological damage, social justice, peacemaking, development, or developing creative worship might have some idea where to start, if they haven't already. The list is just a sample which might be helpful.

Christianity today manifests itself in many more ways than what are obviously churches. There are many other bodies which are part of the whole movement. Christian organizations for social action are able to work through issues with a specified and declared Christian perspective, and focus on particular tasks or issues in a way that churches are often unable to do. Having specific Christian groups tackling issues can sometimes be helpful for a campaign or project. But sometimes it is unhelpful having several organizations working at the same task. One might be more effective. Many Christians are involved in both overt Christian organizations and others with a more mixed membership.

My view is that, whatever kind of organization people get involved in, they still need to weigh up for themselves what is going on, to use their own judgement about what to pursue and support, and decide what in the organization needs challenge or criticism. And this is the case whether the body concerned is a loose-knit campaign, a task-focused organization, a pressure group, a support network or a church. Living faith will involve both thinking and acting.

At the beginning of this book we thought of a dancer as being a symbol of wisdom, like the ancient Hebrew wisdom continually at play within the world. A dancer must both listen to the music and also be aware of their body's movement within the space around. Moment by moment the dancer's attention will shift from one to the other. There is a double focus here that is like the sight of the owl or the sound of the stereo.

The sight of the owl enables it to hunt and survive. The stereo fills a room with music. The double focus of sound and space enables the dancer to move with the music. What the writers on wisdom were concerned about was not just producing a set of right ideas but describing a way of living well. In the same way that a person cannot learn to dance simply from a book, living well and developing wisdom must involve listening and thinking, and also decisions and action.

What I have set out in this book is meant to be an introduction. Following it up can take two directions; one is to continue to work at the ideas and the thinking. There might be questions to pursue or issues which are opened up and call for further explorations. The arguments presented here are very brief and there might be a need to consider these in more depth before either accepting them or writing them off. And there might be the simple matter of pure curiosity or intellectual creativity which leads to a desire to continue thinking things through; here the recommended further reading might help.

The other direction is into action or involvement; after all Jesus was not fundamentally concerned with helping people answer their questions. He was concerned with trying to get people to see things in a new light, and to live in a new way. What he called for was faith, and whilst faith calls for exploration and thinking it is not so much something one has, as something one lives. It is not so much a matter of ideas, as of attitude and action.

APPENDIX A
FURTHER READING

This appendix is for readers who might want to take some of the ideas in this book a bit further or to explore the background. The books listed cover a wide range of subjects and are of different kinds. A few notes are given on each book to help give some idea of what that particular title is about and what it is like.

Chapter 1: Key Images

William Montgomery Watt, *Religious Truth for our Time* (Oneworld Publications, Oxford) 1995; a brief and down-to-earth study of the nature of truth in religion.

Ian G Barbour, *Myths, Models and Paradigms: the nature of scientific and religious language* (SCM, London) 1974; a clear, technical study of the use of key images and stories in religion and science.

J Bronowski, *The Ascent of Man* (BBC, London) 1973; a history of the development of human understanding of the world, presenting the key images of different periods.

Yvonne Burgess, *The Myth of Progress* (Wild Goose Publications, Glasgow) 1996; a reflection on one of the key images of Western culture in the light of the impact it has had on the rest of the world.

Chapter 2: Knowledge, Skill and Wisdom

Bernhard W. Anderson, *The Living World of the Old Testament* (Longmans, Green & Co, London) 2nd Edition, 1968 and Howard Clark Kee and Franklin W Young, *The Living World of the New Testament*

(Darton, Longman & Todd, London) 1960; substantial and readable books setting out the historical backgound to the Bible.

Etienne Charpentier, *How to Read the Old Testament* (SCM, London) 1982, and Etienne Charpentier, *How to Read the New Testament* (SCM, London) 1982; guidebooks to the Old and New Testaments, with both detailed study and overviews.

Gabriel Moran, *Education Toward Adulthood: Religion and Lifelong Learning* (Gill & Macmillan, Dublin) 1979; a book which argues that educationalists should recognise that there are different kinds of learning and that these continue throughout life.

Thomas H Groome, *Christian Religious Education: Sharing our Story and Vision* (Harper & Row, San Francisco) 1980; a detailed book providing a theoretical basis for Christian learning which integrates insight and practice.

Anthony de Mello, *One Minute Wisdom* (Doubleday, New York) 1986; stories from the world's religions: wise and often funny.

Chapter 3: The Planet and the Cosmos

Ghillean T Prance, *The Earth under Threat: A Christian perspective* (Wild Goose Publications, Glasgow, 1996); a basic book from the director of Kew Gardens which draws on his scientific knowledge and the Christian tradition to give insight and practical suggestions.

Celia Deane Drummond, *A Handbook in Theology and Ecology* (SCM, London) 1996; produced by the WWF Religion and Ecology project.

Ian Bradley, *God is Green: Christianity and the Environment* (Darton, Longman and Todd, London) 1990; a short book which draws on modern science and theology to present both a way of seeing the world and practical suggestions for the churches.

Tim Cooper, *Green Christians: caring for the whole creation* (Hodder & Stoughton, London) 1990; written by an economist and ecological consultant.

Chapter 4: Between Two Worlds

Gerd Theissen, *The Shadow of the Galilean* (SCM, London) 1987; a New Testament scholar applies his imagination and his knowledge to retell the story of Jesus.

James D G Dunn, *Jesus' call to Discipleship* (Cambridge University Press); a basic and readable book by the professor of theology at Durham University.

Thomas A Harris, *I'm OK, You're OK* (Pan Books, London) 1973; a popular introduction to Transactional Analysis.

Jean C Morrison, *A Tool for Christians*, Book 1 (Dept of Education, Church of Scotland, Edinburgh) 4th Edition 1993; a basic book to teach the use of Transactional Analysis.

Chapter 5: The Cycle of Healing

Amy and Thomas Harris, *Staying OK* (Pan Books, London) 1986; the sequel to *I'm OK, You're OK*, with less theory and more practice.

Jean C Morrison, *A Tool for Christians*, Book 2 (Dept of Education, Church of Scotland, Edinburgh) 4th Edition 1983; the sequel to book 1: more detail, taking the insights further.

Kathy Galloway, *Imagining the Gospels* (SPCK, London) 1988; a number of incidents involving Jesus are looked at from inside the story.

Frank Lake, *Clinical Theology : A Theological and Psychological Basis to Clinical Pastoral Care* (Darton, Longman & Todd, London) Abridged edition 1986; a detailed and heavy work which argues that a cycle of care is essential for growth and healing.

Chapter 6: Violence and Jesus' Third Way

Elias Chacour, *Blood Brothers* (Kingsway, Eastbourne) 1984; a Christian Palestinian who is committed to peaceful change and reconciliation tells his story.

Martin Luther King, *Strength to Love* (Hodder & Stoughton, London) 1964; sermons by one of the century's great leaders and teachers of nonviolence.

Walter Wink, *Engaging the Powers* (Augsburg Fortress, Minneapolis) 1992; a thorough study of the way that destructive systems can be challenged creatively.

John Howard Yoder, *The Politics of Jesus* (Paternoster Press, Carlisle) revised edition 1994; looks at the way Jesus taught and lived out creative nonviolence

Chapter 7: Play and the Life of the Spirit

John V Taylor, *The Go-Between God: The Holy Spirit and Christian Mission* (SCM, London) 1972; a classic book by a creative theologian who has been a missionary, a bishop and chairman of the Church of England's Doctrine Commission.

Steve Shaw, *Dancing with your Shadow* (SPCK, London) 1995; a short and straightforward book by a theologian and counsellor drawing on the insights of C G Jung.

James Roose-Evans, *Passages of the Soul: Rediscovering the Importance of Rituals in Everyday Life* (Element, Shaftesbury) 1994; a dramatist applies his experience of theatre and God to understanding rituals and creating new ones.

Matthew Fox, *Original Blessing: a Primer in Creation Spirituality* (Bear & Co., Santa Fe, New Mexico) 1983; a fast and compact book which argues that Christian thinking should begin with creation and sketches out a pattern for creative living.

Chapter 8: Living Faith

Ian M Fraser, *Strange Fire* (Wild Goose Publications, Glasgow) 1994; life stories and prayers.

Francis Dewar, *Live for a Change: Discovering and Using your gifts* (Darton, Longman & Todd, London) 1988; a handbook with practical exercises.

Gerard W Hughes, *God of Surprises* (Darton, Longman & Todd, London) 2nd Edition 1996; a widely selling book which has helped a lot of people discover new things about themselves and God.

John D Davies, *Creed and Conflict* (Lutterworth Press, Cambridge) 1979; the Apostles' Creed as a way of seeing the world and living politically within it.

APPENDIX B
GROUPS, MAGAZINES AND ORGANIZATIONS

This appendix is for readers who want to get more involved with other people in tackling some of the issues we face as a society, as well as or apart from belonging to a church. Often people will do that within their local community or their work situation, but some also want to get together with others who are thinking and working along similar lines. The list below is a small selection of groups and organisations which are tackling issues raised in this book. Information on many others and on local groups is generally available in public libraries.

Campaign Against the Arms Trade, 11 Goodwin Street, London, N4 3HQ (0171-281-0297); campaigning body aiming to reduce the destructive international trade in weapons.

Campaign for Nuclear Disarmament, and *Christian CND*, 162 Holloway Road, London N7 8DQ; working for the removal of nuclear weapons.

Centre for Alternative Technology, Machynlleth, Powys, SY20 9AZ (01654-703743); experiments, courses and information on green technologies.

Christian Aid, PO Box 100, London SE1 7RT (0171-620-4444), and 41 George IV Bridge, Edinburgh, EH1 1EL (0131-220-1254); the churches' world development and relief organisation.

Christian Ecology Link, 20 Carlton Road, Harrogate, North Yorkshire (01423-871616); a network of Christians with green concerns.

Christian magazine, 19 Harvey Road, Guildford, GU1 3SE; quarterly publication, subtitled 'Living for a Change'.

Clinical Theology Association, St Mary's House, Church Westcote, Oxford, OX7 6SF; publications and courses which integrate psychology, psychotherapy and Christian faith.

Corrymeela Community, 8 Upper Crescent, Belfast, BT7 1NT; Catholic and Protestant Christians working for reconciliation and the healing of the social, political and religious divisions in Ireland and throughout the world.

Council of Churches in Britain and Ireland, Inter-Church House, 35-41 Lower Marsh, London, SE1 7RL; co-ordinating body for discussion and joint action by the different churches.

Centre for Creation Spirituality, St James's Church, 197 Piccadilly, London, W1V 9LF; encouraging and promoting prayer, worship and action which takes Creation seriously.

Friends of the Earth (England), 26-28 Underwood Street, London N1 7JQ (0171-490-1555), and *Friends of the Earth* (Scotland), 72 Newhaven Road, Edinburgh EH6 5QG (0131-554-9977; information and campaign organisations.

Greenbelt, The Greenhouse, P.O. Box 1335, Birkenhead L41 8GB; annual Christian arts festival with seminars, workshops, talks and exploration of life issues.

Greenpeace, Canonbury Villas, London, N1 2PN; high profile environmental campaigners.

The Iona Community, Pearce Institute, 840 Govan Road, Glasgow, G51 3UU (0141-445-4561); Christian community aiming to bring together work and worship, prayer and politics, the sacred and the secular.

National Retreat Association, The Central Hall, 256 Bermondsey Street, London, SE1 3UJ; journal *The Vision* lists retreats and courses on a wide range of forms of spirituality.

New Internationalist, 55 Rectory Road, Oxford, OX4 1BW (01865-728181); magazine on issues of justice and world development.

One World Week, PO Box 100, London SE1 7RT; the week is an annual occasion for reflection and action on global issues, promoted by the British churches and involving thousands of people. The office can provide information all year round.

Pax Christi, 9 Henry Road, London N4 2LH (0181-800-4612); working to bring Christ's peace to the world through nonviolence.

Peace House, The Old Manse, Greenloaning, Perthshire, FK15 0NB (01786-880490); courses and information on dealing creatively with violent actions and structures.

Student Christian Movement, Westhill College, 14-16 Wesley Park Road, Selly Oak, Birmingham B29 6LL (0121-471-2404); aims to offer students a caring, thoughtful environment in local groups at colleges and universities, holds conferences and publishes a magazine: Movement.

The Taizé Community, 71250 Cluny, France ((33) 385 50 30 02); provides a place of meeting for young adults from all over the world where there is a chance to think more deeply about what counts for them and to share their searching with people from different backgrounds.

Traidcraft, Team Valley Estate, Kingsway, Gateshead, NE11 0NE (0191-491-0591); trading organisation aiming to provide market opportunities and a just reward for Third World producers

Westminster Pastoral Foundation, 23 Kensington Square, London W8 5HN; aiming to provide facilities and training in counselling.

World Development Movement, 25 Beehive Place, London, SW9 7QR (0171-737-6215); information and campaigning organisation for justice in world trade.

The Iona Community

The Iona Community is an ecumenical Christian community, founded in 1938 by the late Lord MacLeod of Fuinary (the Rev. George MacLeod DD) and committed to seeking new ways of living the Gospel in today's world. Gathered around the rebuilding of the ancient monastic buildings of Iona Abbey, but with its original inspiration in the poorest areas of Glasgow during the Depression, the Community has sought ever since the 'rebuilding of the common life', bringing together work and worship, prayer and politics, the sacred and the secular in ways that reflect its strongly incarnational theology.

The Community today is a movement of some 200 Members, over 1,400 Associate Members and about 1,600 Friends. The Members — women and men from many backgrounds and denominations, most in Britain, but some overseas — are committed to a rule of daily prayer and Bible reading, sharing and accounting for their use of time and money, regular meeting and action for justice and peace.

The Iona Community maintains three centres on Iona and Mull: Iona Abbey and the MacLeod Centre on Iona, and Camas Adventure Camp on the Ross of Mull. Its base is in Community House, Glasgow, where it also supports work with young people, the Wild Goose Resource and Worship Groups, a bimonthly magazine (*Coracle*) and a publishing house (Wild Goose Publications).

For further information on the Iona Community please contact:

The Iona Community,
Pearce Institute,
840 Govan Road,
Glasgow
G51 3UU

T. 0141 445 4561; F. 0141 445 4295
e-mail: ionacomm@gla.iona.org.uk

OTHER TITLES FROM WGP

SONGBOOKS with full music (titles marked * have companion cassettes)
WHEN GRIEF IS RAW, John Bell and Graham Maule
THE LAST JOURNEY - PACK OF 15 OCTAVOS* John Bell
THE LAST JOURNEY reflections*, John Bell
THE COURAGE TO SAY NO: 23 SONGS FOR EASTER & LENT*John Bell
and Graham Maule
GOD NEVER SLEEPS – PACK OF 12 OCTAVOS* John Bell
COME ALL YOU PEOPLE, Shorter Songs for Worship* John Bell
PSALMS OF PATIENCE, PROTEST AND PRAISE* John Bell
HEAVEN SHALL NOT WAIT (Wild Goose Songs Vol.1)* J Bell & Graham Maule
ENEMY OF APATHY (Wild Goose Songs Vol.2) J Bell & Graham Maule
LOVE FROM BELOW (Wild Goose Songs Vol.3)* John Bell & Graham Maule
INNKEEPERS & LIGHT SLEEPERS* (for Christmas) John Bell
MANY & GREAT (Songs of the World Church Vol.1)* John Bell (ed./arr.)
SENT BY THE LORD (Songs of the World Church Vol.2)* John Bell (ed./arr.)
FREEDOM IS COMING* Anders Nyberg (ed.)
PRAISING A MYSTERY, Brian Wren
BRING MANY NAMES, Brian Wren

CASSETTES & CDs (titles marked † have companion songbooks)
CD, THE LAST JOURNEY, † John Bell (guest conductor)
Tape, THE LAST JOURNEY, † John Bell (guest conductor)
Tape, IONA ABBEY, WORSHIP FROM EASTER WEEK (ed/arr Steve Butler)
Tape, THE COURAGE TO SAY NO † Wild Goose Worship Group
Tape, GOD NEVER SLEEPS † John Bell (guest conductor)
CD, GOD NEVER SLEEPS † John Bell (guest conductor)
Tape, COME ALL YOU PEOPLE † Wild Goose Worship Group
CD, PSALMS OF PATIENCE, PROTEST AND PRAISE † Wild Goose Worship
Group
Tape, PSALMS OF PATIENCE, PROTEST AND PRAISE † WGWG
Tape, HEAVEN SHALL NOT WAIT † Wild Goose Worship Group
Tape, LOVE FROM BELOW † Wild Goose Worship Group
Tape, INNKEEPERS & LIGHT SLEEPERS † (for Christmas) WGWG
Tape, SENT BY THE LORD † Wild Goose Worship Group
Tape, FREEDOM IS COMING † Fjedur
Tape, TOUCHING PLACE, A, Wild Goose Worship Group
Tape, CLOTH FOR THE CRADLE, Wild Goose Worship Group

DRAMA BOOKS
EH JESUS...YES PETER No. 1, John Bell and Graham Maule
EH JESUS...YES PETER No. 2, John Bell and Graham Maule
EH JESUS...YES PETER No. 3, John Bell and Graham Maule

PRAYER/WORSHIP BOOKS
THE PILGRIMS' MANUAL, Christopher Irvine
THE PATTERN OF OUR DAYS, Kathy Galloway (ed.)
PRAYERS AND IDEAS FOR HEALING SERVICES, Ian Cowie
HE WAS IN THE WORLD: Meditations for Public Worship, John Bell
EACH DAY AND EACH NIGHT: Prayers from Iona in the Celtic Tradition, Philip Newell
IONA COMMUNITY WORSHIP BOOK,
THE WHOLE EARTH SHALL CRY GLORY, George MacLeod

OTHER BOOKS
COLUMBA: Pilgrim and Penitent, Ian Bradley
THE EARTH UNDER THREAT: A Christian Perspective, Ghillean Prance
THE MYTH OF PROGRESS, Yvonne Burgess
WHAT IS THE IONA COMMUNITY?
PUSHING THE BOAT OUT: New Poetry, Kathy Galloway (ed.)
EXILE IN ISRAEL: A Personal Journey with the Palestinians, Runa Mackay
FALLEN TO MEDIOCRITY: CALLED TO EXCELLENCE, Erik Cramb
REINVENTING THEOLOGY AS THE PEOPLE'S WORK, Ian Fraser

WILD GOOSE ISSUES/REFLECTIONS
A VERY BRITISH MONSTER: A Challenge to UK Immigration Policy, Stanley Hope
A FAREWELL TO THE ARMS TRADE, Bernadette Meaden
CELEBRATING SAINTS: Augustine, Columba, Ninian, Ian Fraser
COMPASSION IN THE MARKETPLACE, Joy Mead
SURPLUS BAGGAGE: The Apostles' Creed, Ralph Smith
THE APOSTLES' CREED: A Month of Meditations, David Levison
WOMEN TOGETHER, Ena Wyatt & Rowsan Malik